# Heaven is Near...
# When a Child Dies

One mother's choice

to **embrace** her son's spiritual **life**

while **grieving** his physical **death**

Lori Hoflen

JHL Inc.
Elk Horn, Iowa

Heaven is Near… When a Child Dies

Copyright © 2012 by Lori Hoflen

Published by JHL Inc.
4314 Main St., Elk Horn, Iowa 51531

All rights reserved. No part of this publication may be reproduced, stored in a retrieval system, or transmitted in any form by any means, electronic, mechanical, photocopy, recording, or otherwise, without the prior permission of the publisher, except as provided for by USA copyright law.

Cover design: Lori Hoflen
Cover illustration: Lori Hoflen
Author photo of Lori Hoflen by Fischer Photography

First printing 2012
Printed in the United States of America

Unless otherwise noted, Scripture quotations contained herein are from the New Revised Standard Version Bible, copyright, 1989, by the Division of Christian Education of the National Council of the Churches of Christ in the USA. Used by permission. All rights reserved.

All emphasis in Scripture quotations have been added by the author.

ISBN 978-0-9845007-0-3

# This book is dedicated to...

**The Glory of the Blessed Holy Trinity —**
   **God** our gracious Heavenly Father,
   our Lord and Savior **Jesus Christ**,
   and the **Holy Spirit**, whose profound gifts and indwelling I do not deserve, but am forever thankful.

**Jim, my beloved husband and steadfast friend, and our eleven children** whom we have devoted the rest of our lives to loving unconditionally, caring for physically, and nurturing their faith spiritually.

**All those who have suffered the harsh travels deep within the valley of the shadow of death.** I lift you up in prayer, and am giving you permission to borrow my faith for as long as yours is hanging by a thread. Graciously allow yourself to grieve, but not to become stuck within that valley. Trust that God's grace is sufficient and that your loved one's spiritual life is beautiful to embrace.

# Psalm 23

The LORD is my Shepherd, I shall not want.
    He makes me lie down in green pastures;
He leads me beside still waters;
    He restores my soul.
He leads me in paths of righteousness
    for His name's sake.
**Even though I walk through the valley of the shadow of death,**
    **I fear no evil;**
    **for You are with me;**
    Your rod and Your staff —
    they comfort me.
You prepare a table before me in the presence of my enemies;
    You anoint my head with oil;
    my cup overflows.
Surely goodness and mercy shall follow me
    all the days of my life,
    and I shall dwell in the house of the LORD
    my whole life long.

# John 16:20-24

[20] "Very truly, I tell you, you will weep and mourn...; you will have pain, but your pain will turn into joy.

[21] When a woman is in labor, she has pain, because her hour has come. But when her child is born, she no longer remembers the anguish because of the joy of having brought a human being into the world.

[22] So you have pain now, but I will see you again, and your hearts will rejoice, and no one will take your joy from you.

[23] ...Very truly, I tell you, if you ask anything of the Father in My name, He will give it to you.

[24] ...**Ask and you will receive, so that your joy may be complete.**"

## Matthew 28:18-20

[18] And Jesus came and said to them, "All authority in heaven and on earth has been given to me.
[19] Go therefore and make disciples of all nations, baptizing them in the name of the Father and of the Son and of the Holy Spirit,
[20] and teaching them to obey everything that I have commanded you. And **remember, I am with you always, to the end of the age.**"

# Contents

Prologue..................9
The Miracle Baby..................11
The Phone Call..................19
Grief..................27
Gratitude..................41
Love Connection..................47
Saying Goodbye..................65
Going Home..................81
God Is With Us..................95
Comfort..................105
Insanity..................113
Answered Prayers..................127
Embarrassment..................135
The Power of Pictures..................147
A Difficult Decision..................159
More Decisions..................171
Rollercoaster Emotions..................179
Frenzied Preparations..................189
Celebration of Life..................203
Epilogue..................219
About the Author..................223
About Hoflen Ministries..................224

# Prologue

The events of this book took place over the course of just eight days in March, 2007. Within three weeks, the majority of this book was written. Why did it take until now to get published? The simple answer is that I am not a writer. I have never published a book before. The process of getting it ready to be published and a busy family schedule is what has taken so long.

My husband, Jim, has been incredible with setting up the company to publish this book and also our ministry, as well as being my shoulder to cry on when the going was so very difficult.

This book has been written by me, from a mom's perspective. Jim and others provided suggestions and support for which I'm extremely grateful. This book was originally intended to include Jim's perspective as a dad, but we decided he will write a separate book in the future.

Only one event in this book has been modified. Zaeden's favorite book that our family read to him countless times contains colorful animals, such as a brown bear and a green frog. That popular children's book is the one I recited from memory during the last minutes of Zaeden's life here on earth. However, that author/publisher denied us permission to place the words in this book due to their copyright restrictions. I was devastated because I wanted this book to be entirely accurate and true to the events that occurred.

When explaining this disappointment to Jim and the kids, we brainstormed the exciting idea to write Zaeden his own very special book. "Zaeden's Rainbow" resulted. The kids played a major part in deciding the colors and animals. I researched children's books and put the story in order. Adriel illustrated it by creating pencil drawings of the characters. I spent countless hours with my computer software converting the scanned in pencil drawings into colorful book pages. Now I understand how challenging it is not only to write a book but also to illustrate one!

While designing the back cover for "Zaeden's Rainbow," I understood that the negative experience with that author/publisher is the essence of "Heaven is Near… When a Child Dies."

Life is so harsh sometimes. Being angry and devastated is a normal reaction. At some point though, it needs to be squarely faced and dealt with. God knows each of us intimately because he made us. He will help each of us through our life challenges, whether big or small. The choice each of us must make is whether we allow the harsh event to define us, or allow God to walk with us in dealing with it so we can see the beauty of a rainbow after the darkness of a storm.

I am humbled that you would read this book and pray blessings may be poured out to you from these pages.

                                        peace,
                                        lori

# The Miracle Baby

Having birthed 11 children, I understand that tears of joy, as well as pain, can accompany a miracle, especially the miracle of childbirth.

When our youngest son Zaeden was born, my husband Jim and I were told that he was a miracle child. I was almost 43 and he was our tenth child, born unexpectedly at home, with no complications, and was normal and healthy. Neither of us fathomed that Zaeden's birth was just the beginning of the miracles we would experience with him.

Imagine what our family life is like every minute of every day. Quiet time doesn't exist, except perhaps for a few hours in the middle of the night. During waking hours, there is a constant buzz of sibling rivalry, parental discipline, and household appliances toiling endlessly for our convenience. It may appear to an outsider that we live in constant chaos, but to us it is just a normal day.

Our home is too small for a family our size, but the cramped quarters have allowed a complex connection to evolve between each of us. When our older kids have friends over, it is often the younger kids who are the entertainment for them. The middle kids

get away with almost anything and cover for each other because they know the younger ones are usually blamed and the older ones are held accountable.

We have what we call "public" areas of the house – the living room, dining room, kitchen, and bathroom – and we all know that if something is left in those areas you may never see it again. That's just our life.

We don't stress over the messiness, and we don't even attempt to have everything written on the calendar because in one second it can all be turned upside down. We live in the moment that is now.

It is, I've found, the only and best way to live this life we know so little of in this world.

The small farming community of Elk Horn, Iowa, is home for us, and where our kids all attend the community school that is contained in one city block. From pre-school through high school, the kids have a good social structure with perhaps 25 other kids in their grade. They play with their siblings at recess time if they want to, wave at each other in the hallways, and eat with their friends and siblings in the same cafeteria. The high school kids are helpers for the pre-school and elementary classes. They've been able to thrive in a good educational environment, and they've been able to participate in a lot of extra-curricular activities.

We are active Christians, and we're members of our local church. I am a volunteer EMT with our local rescue squad, coach volleyball, teach Sunday school, and have a Master's Degree in Software Engineering.

Jim is retired from the Air Force, but is active in the American Legion, taking part in gun salutes for veterans' funerals. He represents the Air Force in our community's annual Tivoli Memorial Day parade and festivities. His priority for our kids has been supporting their education, and

he was instrumental in the decision-making and fundraising for our huge school building addition in 2002.

Jim usually stays home to care for the younger children while I attend the older children's sports events, and I stay home with the younger children while Jim attends the children's band, choir concerts and theatre events. It works out well for all of us.

Jim and I both worked full-time during the majority of the years we've been married. Exhaustion, excitement, confusion, cell phone minutes and mileage have usually been off the charts. Fortunately, in 2006, we both found work at the same company just across the street from our house. Jim was the Director of IT Infrastructure and I was an IT Project Manager.

Our house is in town, only four blocks from the school, but we also own a farm about four miles away with farm animals, vegetable and flower gardens, and a small vineyard. For Jim and me, the farm is our safe  haven, a refuge where the kids have enough space to run around and play, and yet there's always a spot that's relatively quiet. The children often equate being at the  farm with work, and do a fair amount of complaining about it, yet they enjoy the hot dog roasts and bonfires, playing volleyball and tetherball, and just running free through the grasses and woods of the farm. Our dream is to someday move our house to the farm.

 With so many kids, our house is filled with lots of noise, chaos, and love. The dishes are never all done and there are always at least six loads of laundry waiting to be washed. We have one washing machine, one

dryer, a broken dishwasher, and a drain in the basement that routinely gets clogged and soaks our laundry room floor.

The kids' friends are welcome day or night. I call the kids' friends my children as well, and they blend in with the traffic flow

throughout our house. We never mind setting an extra plate, or two, or three at mealtime.

I make the rounds at bedtime to count the kids and make sure they are all safely home, reminding them to say their prayers. Jim and I wouldn't have it any other way.

Our family's crazy, chaotic schedule was slammed to a halt, however, one evening as

Jim and I attended the winter sports banquet at school. My cell phone rang and my daughter frantically told me that she thought Zaeden, our two-year-old son, was choking.

From that moment, all of our lives changed. Our family experienced what every parent dreads, and none of us expects to happen.

But, it did happen, and as I said before, we could never have fathomed the love, and pain, and joy, and peace that have been intertwined with the miracles that God gifted to us through Zaeden. Because these miracles occur so frequently now we simply call them blessings, and are eternally appreciative.

In sharing Zaeden's story, we hope you may be blessed, as well.

# The Phone Call

Tuesday evening, March 20, 2007, Jim and I, as well as our sons Nolan, Chandler, and Kael were attending a sports banquet in the high school cafeteria where Nolan and Chandler would be recognized for their accomplishments in varsity and junior varsity basketball. I'd been to almost every one of our kids' games wherever they played, camera in hand, supporting their various God-given talents as best I could. The cafeteria was crowded with parents who were all just as proud of their kids as Jim and I were proud of ours. Now, I settled back into my seat, beaming with pride.

We had decided to keep Kael, age 12, at home until the awards were ready to be handed out. That way he could feed the younger three boys at home and Adriel, age 10, and Grace, age nine, could eat at the banquet with us. Then Jim took Adriel and Grace home to watch the younger three while the awards were handed out, and brought Kael to watch the award ceremony. Both girls knew all about caring for their little brothers, including bath time, changing diapers, fixing simple meals, and cleaning up after them. Every child in our family had learned to pitch in whenever needed.

I thought back to the morning, where our normal routine was for Jim to leave for work at 7:00 a.m. and then come back home at 8:00 a.m. to help me get the final round of chaos settled down before getting our older kids off to school and our two little guys to the babysitter just down the street. It had been a good morning. Zaeden, age two, and Macrae, age three, woke up a bit grumpy, but very cuddly as Jim and I got them dressed. By the time we got their coats on they were wide-awake and happy to be going to their sitter. Angie is a caring mom, and she loved our two just as her own. Each day she had a new story of what fun they'd had or a new color Zaeden had learned, or something silly Macrae had said. I knew they were in a safe, loving home while I was at work.

The company I worked for, and our sitter, offered the flexibility that I could occasionally work from home. I knew all too well the toll taken not just on me, but our whole family, when I worked long days in an office, then traveled an hour to and from home over the past many years. So those days I could work from home, I did just that, and often had the little guys curled up beside me with my computer, while they drew or played with Legos. Those days were happy, memorable, and cherished.

Applause brought my attention back to the coach and the wrestlers he was recognizing. Jim heard his cell phone and saw that he had just missed a call from home, so he went out of the cafeteria to call the kids. Just then my cell phone rang, and I saw that it was from home. The reception wasn't good in the cafeteria so I quickly went outside. As I struggled to hear Grace, I understood that she was frantically trying to tell me that she thought Zaeden was choking. I screamed for Jim, but he didn't answer. I didn't know where our car was parked, so my quickest way home was to run the four blocks to our house. I told Grace to have Adriel take Zaeden outside to get help and then call 911. I was on my way home. I knew that Jim would be right behind me.

I frantically looked up and down the street, hoping to see a car to get me home faster, but none was in sight. I began to run as fast as I could. When I looked back again I saw a car coming my direction. Waving her down, I urged the driver to rush me home. The car was still moving when I jumped out at our house. Grace met me outside and said Adriel had taken Zaeden next door for help. I sprinted to that neighbor's and saw that Zaeden was gasping for air, but had a solid heart rate.

As a volunteer EMT with our local rescue squad, I'd been recently recertified in CPR. I knew from my initial assessment that it was a terrible situation. I couldn't see anything in his throat, and my back blows didn't dislodge what was choking him. He went unconscious. I switched to chest compressions, and then ran outside with him to meet the ambulance.

Inside the ambulance, we immediately noted that he no longer had a pulse. The EMT in the ambulance continued chest compressions. A paramedic did the airway examination and saw an object deep in his throat. Reaching in with forceps, he miraculously managed to pull out a piece of fruit. We administered oxygen with airway support and chest compressions until we reached the hospital. The heart monitor displayed a very slow heart rate. I knew from the assessment I did during that ride that Zaeden was not going to survive.

 The staff in the ER was prepared for our arrival, and they delivered medication in an attempt to jump-start and stabilize his heart. His heart stabilized, and he started breathing again, first erratically, and then settling in at a slow rate. Jim arrived at the hospital and said he had arranged for someone to watch the kids.

 We weren't able to have the Life Flight helicopter fly Zaeden to Omaha due to the fog that evening, but we rushed him to Omaha by ambulance, with me riding along. Jim called Taralyn and Schuyler, who were away at college, and then followed the ambulance to Omaha.

 We were met with a team of personnel at the hospital who quickly assessed the situation, and stabilized Zaeden's breathing with a ventilator. They began a series of tests to further determine the situation. By then, I already knew the prognosis. I was completely emotionally and physically overwhelmed with the grief of knowing that my baby was dying.

 As the staff did the rest of the testing, I waited with Jim in the waiting room. Soon our family began arriving. As the minutes went on, my mind lost ability to reason. I cried uncontrollably, and went to the floor on my knees in grief. I could not stand, I could not sit, and I could not be still, yet I could not move. I have never, ever, felt such agony. How do you bury a baby?

I cursed and yelled at God for abandoning me when I'd found Zaeden. I'd had a strong faith, but now I was so angry with God because He did not let me dislodge the fruit when I first found Zaeden. If he had, Zaeden could have survived. And I knew in my heart, before any test results were presented to us that Zaeden, my baby son, was dying.

I was in Hell. Those hours were filled with my rocking back and forth with grief that could not be comforted, although Jim tried. My sisters, Sandy and Julee, and my brother, Greg, arrived and they talked to me and held me. One of the doctors said that the test results showed a better prognosis than they had first thought and that through the night they would know more about his long-term condition. I accused the doctor of giving us false hope and I was angry. So angry that I couldn't be calmed. So scared that I couldn't be comforted. So lonely that I shut out God and everyone else.

Our pastor arrived and prayed with us, listened, and offered comfort, asking if he or anyone else in the congregation could do anything else for us. At one point, he knelt in front of me and looked me in the eyes. "What do you see in my eyes?" he asked.

I replied, "Caring." He nodded, but added, "and hope." I simply replied that no, I didn't see any hope. I didn't. I knew better than to hope. Zaeden was not going to live. I knew that. I realized I was the only one without hope, and that made me feel even worse. I grew frustrated with their futile words and their praying for a lost cause.

As soon as the nurse told us the testing was finished for the evening, Jim and I went to be with Zaeden. So many tubes and so many machines connected to his small body. I looked past all that, though, and saw my baby, pink and warm, lying in bed as though he were asleep. The ventilator kept his breathing at a steady rate, and the heart monitor showed a strong heartbeat. I touched him tenderly and talked to him. I knew he could hear me. I knew it. I could feel it.

Another wave of grief overwhelmed me and my thoughts turned inward. I felt the need to stay with Zaeden. Not just to be physically with him in the hospital, but with him as he was dying. I felt that because God had abandoned me during my deepest need for Him, that the world now just consisted of Zaeden and me, and that Zaeden needed me with him. I needed to be with him, too. I longed to take him in my arms and comfort him. It was difficult, however, to even find a place to hold onto him because he had IV lines and monitor lines all over his little body. Looking at him and touching him wherever I could, I cried and cried. Jim tried to comfort me, but I couldn't be comforted.

During that night, I realized my sisters and brothers were worried about whether or not *I* would pull through. They pointed out that I didn't have tears anymore, and that I was dehydrated. What they didn't realize was that I no longer felt alive. Part of me was dying with Zaeden.

I didn't care. So empty, so angry, so forsaken – I felt like a nothing. I had no worth, I was unworthy of God's presence when I most needed Him, and I no longer felt reason to be physically alive. I did not eat, and when my sisters and brother gave me sips of water, dry heaves felt as if I was being ripped apart from inside. My heart was broken, shattered, ripped into shreds.

As my sister Sandy and I sat with Zaeden, I gently held onto the bottom of his leg. I put my head down onto the bed and cried as softly as I could because I wanted him to rest as much as possible. My sisters sat on the opposite side of the bed with Zaeden lying between us. Our grief was tangible, powerfully connecting us.

As we cried and caressed Zaeden, and spoke loving words to him, my sister pointed to a tear that trickled down Zaeden's cheek. I stared at that clear drop of his being as it rolled down his cheek, the first sign that he was still with us. The clarity of that teardrop opened my eyes to his grieving with us that he was dying physically. I realized that he hadn't wanted to leave us and that he was desperately trying to live. I comforted him and knew that he and I were still connected as mother and son. The power of that connection went all through my being.

I remembered being pregnant with him and the wonder of his birth and the cord being cut to give him his own separate life from me. I longed for that physical connection while I was still pregnant, eating healthy foods, directly in control of caring for him and nurturing him. I wanted him safe inside of me again, being cared for constantly, our hearts so close to each other. I only felt empty, my womb old and useless to him.

As powerful waves of grief rolled through me, I needed to back away from him because I didn't want to disturb him. Having seen him shed a tear when I was so distraught forced a realization that he could hear me and feel my grief. I couldn't bear to have him know that I wasn't able to care for him and be strong for him. I remembered his bumps, cuts, and bruises, and as Doctor Mom I always bandaged him and kissed the pain away. Ashamed of my grief, I leaned on the wall for support, but felt nothing supporting me. I went to the floor on my knees, curled up in a fetal position and in excruciating pain. The floor was the only place I could go, down to the lowest point of my physical existence.

Even as the waves of anguish consumed me, I wrestled with the maternal need to be next to my dying son. Again and again I went to him, caressed his head, held his hand, and talked with him, assuring him that I was with him and that I would never leave him. I gasped for air, unable to breathe, hyperventilating and deprived of oxygen simultaneously. It was hell. Darkness, hopelessness, and death were constants.

I longed to hold my son, to scoop him up and see him without all the tubing and wiring. Knowing that he was dying, even though he was pink and warm, was so hard to bear. It was against everything I felt as a mother, to be at the mercy of others to know what to do in caring for what was left of life in my son.

Late the next afternoon, Wednesday, the feedback from the doctor reiterated what I already knew. Test results confirmed that Zaeden only had brain stem activity left. There would be no recovery.

# Grief

Jim, Sandy, Julee, Greg, and the rest of our core group of adults received the results harshly. This whole time they had been clinging to hope and prayer and wanting a miracle. I couldn't look backward at them walking the path where I'd already gone. I kept walking forward into the darkness. I no longer felt as if I wanted to live. I only felt as if I wanted to be with Zaeden. My thoughts turned to holding him forever and in my mind I envisioned me holding him in a shared casket. My mother instinct clung so fiercely to him that it controlled my destiny.

I was told sometime that afternoon that our younger kids were being driven to the hospital and someone had arranged for them to stay at the Rainbow House, a nearby temporary living accommodation for families of critically ill patients. When the kids arrived at the hospital, I could tell that they were trying to grasp what was happening with Zaeden. Our three-year-old, Macrae, simply looked at him and said, "Zaeden sick," and didn't want to be near him. Adriel and Grace had brought books along, and sat next to Zaeden reading to him and talking to him. The older kids could see that Zaeden wasn't awake and realized that the situation was bad. Neither Jim nor I could tell them at that time, though, how bad it was. We let them be happy to see Zaeden, to read to him, to joke with him, to tell him how much they loved him.

So much love pulsed through that hospital room that I knew Zaeden was comforted. I knew his sisters and brothers felt that love, as well. I began to realize that others were coming into the hospital trying to be of help. An aunt brought games for the kids to play; some teammates and classmates of the older kids showed up; and a friend and a niece visited. Several college classmates of our oldest daughter, Taralyn, had come to the hospital to stay with her and help with the kids. The waiting room had an ebb and flow to it with the coming and going of all those people bringing comfort and food.

Late Wednesday evening, my brother Greg and I sat next to Zaeden in the quiet of his room. I had not wanted to leave Zaeden's room and Greg had graciously offered to spend the night with Zaeden and me. One of the nurses asked if I would like to lie down beside Zaeden. I was surprised at the offering. They brought in a bigger bed and I carefully crawled in beside Zaeden. I nestled as close to him as I dared, and the tubing and monitor lines were moved toward the opposite side so that they wouldn't be disturbed. I lay facing him with my knees curled under him. I stroked his face and chest and arms and legs and hair and touched him as much as I could. I talked with him and cried as softly as I could. While I was with him that night, I sensed a closeness that was the pure connectedness of mother and child.

I was so thankful, so incredibly, sincerely thankful, that I'd been allowed to lie next to him. I felt the powerful love between us, and in the dark it seemed we were transported home where he had lain beside me many nights. In fact, Macrae often still slept in our bed, always on my right side, with Zaeden on my left side, cradled between Jim and me. We have a king-sized bed, and there was always enough room.

As I slept in the hospital bed with him that night, I awoke to Zaeden gently pushing his right foot against my leg, something he had regularly done in the night to make sure I was still lying next to him. We called it a foot-check. Macrae just usually thrashed in bed until I awakened and re-oriented him to lying on his pillow and talked to him, telling him I was still there. Zaeden never needed that; a foot-check was enough. When I felt that against my leg, I realized I'd received yet another wondrous sign from him that despite the test results, he was still with us. I lay still, letting his foot rest against my leg the rest of the night.

The next morning, the doctor needed to do more testing. They could not control his fever and his breathing was labored. Blood perfusion was not being effective enough, and I could feel Zaeden fighting for his life with each breath. I realized that Zaeden was doing everything he could to stay with us, and I could do nothing to help. Again, the anguish completely engulfed me.

At some point during that Thursday, Sandy told me that they were taking me to the emergency room. I knew that I was in bad shape, and I realized that if my physical being didn't stabilize I would be admitted to the hospital. I could not eat, and attempts at drinking were immediately met with dry heaves. I knew my family was genuinely concerned about me.

About that time, I lost my sense of balance. The floor was the only place where I knew I wouldn't fall. I was completely exhausted, and physically needed to lean on someone.

Jim and my siblings gathered around me and told me it was time to get an IV to get fluid into my system. I couldn't sit in the wheelchair because the rolling movement had my mind spinning and then nausea set in. I couldn't stand to look at the walls, the floor, or the ceiling as I was being brought to ER. Sandy sat in the wheelchair and held me. I clung to her and closed my eyes, wishing the nausea and spinning would stop. We entered an elevator and I wasn't prepared for the harsh dropping motion. I felt as if I needed to scream and escape my own body.

We finally reached the ER. My sister explained the basic information, and a doctor came in to assess the situation. At that point, I lost my patience, and probably sanity, as well. I cursed and yelled and demanded that the doctor not give me any medication and that if an IV didn't get started soon they should just hand it over to me so I could start the IV myself.

The doctor quickly assured me that he would not give me any medication, just a normal saline solution that is standard for IVs. Even after the IV was started, I cursed and accused the staff of not running it fast enough and that they should've used a bigger gauge needle so it would flow faster.

My mind reverted to quoting Bible stories of Rachel who refused to be comforted because her children were no more, and David mourning the dying state of his son with his wife Bathsheba. On and on, I spoke harshly to God, and used Bible stories against Him, and hated Him for abandoning me. I understood what Jesus felt when He said God had forsaken Him while He was dying on the cross.

I saw the grief in my family and friends as they surrounded me in that emergency room. I was being a horrible patient and knew they were probably close to committing me. After a full liter of fluid had been pushed into my system, I was angry with myself for having needed that, and embarrassed with my state of delirium. I knew that the return wheelchair ride to Zaeden would be more of the mind spinning and nausea, and it was. The spinning of the chair and the angle of a downward floor ramp sent me into a frantic state. I couldn't take it anymore, and cried inconsolably, begging my sisters to let me try to walk.

Instead, my nephew, Tyson, carefully lifted me, and then carried me, walking slowly and gently down the hall. I didn't want that burden on him, but he quietly insisted, so I buried my head into his shoulder and clung to him. I knew I needed to trust him in order to get back to Zaeden.

I watched as Zaeden and the kids had some loving family time that afternoon and evening. The kids were gentle with him. They spoke about happy things with him, telling him about their schoolwork and about happenings with their friends. Each of the kids just naturally went to him after another of them was done talking with him. Just like they've always done with him. He adored them, each of them, and they loved him for how easily he returned their love.

That evening, Jim and I decided that we should tell them more about Zaeden's condition. Minutes later, after we'd gathered the kids in a small side room of the waiting area, Jim explained to them that Zaeden probably didn't have long to live. It was a horrible realization for all of them and they grieved tremendously. Jim and I tried to answer their questions as best we could, but we didn't know much about what to expect when a person dies, either. We all cried together.

After a long while of talking, Jim and I decided that each of the kids should spend some time alone with Zaeden. By then it was around 9:00 p.m. I felt physically strong enough to walk again without any dizziness or nausea, and I left the waiting room area so I could go to Zaeden's room.

I met Sandy just outside the waiting area door. She had terrible news. Zaeden had taken a turn for the worse. His neurological status was deteriorating and his blood pressure was not stable. Jim and I decided that all of the kids and our pastor should be with Zaeden then. The kids were crying. We were all scared.

As we stood around Zaeden, my grief combined with theirs and it filled the hospital room with a desperation and agony that none of us had ever experienced before. That collective grief was awful to behold and partake in. As I grieved with them, I realized my role as Zaeden's mother also included a role as mother to each of the other nine children.

Through this collective grieving of our family, my protective response to my entire family slowly worked its way through me. A sense of responsibility and motherly caring came into my consciousness. I saw that Jim was deeply grieving. That brought yet another realization. I was going to have to become the strong one, now.

Our family was in severe agony and in need of help. After experiencing such overwhelming anguish and grieving the past few days, I couldn't bear to have my children go through that, as well. I needed to protect them from that.

I needed to do something. But, what? Death is so huge and so powerful, and I understood that it was bigger than I could handle. I'd already tried to handle it myself. And knew that I couldn't.

As I stood next to Zaeden, amongst all of my kids and Jim, I realized that if I showed my children that I was angry with God and had isolated myself from Him, that they were likely to go down the same path of hell that I was on. I didn't want that.

But, I had no idea what to say to them. I couldn't think of anything to do. I couldn't save Zaeden. I felt hopelessness and shame at not knowing how to take care of my children. I'd never felt that before. I'd never felt so inadequate. I didn't care about helping myself through this, but I couldn't abandon my children, not any of them. It was time to trust God again.

*Lord, you know what I need to do for my family now. Tell me what to do.*

A strong surge of love began to warm my heart. In utter humility, I quietly let it just flow into me. The warmth thawed my heart. Then a sense of calm caressed me. A blessed peace flowed softly like a river throughout my entire being. I had never felt peace to such a depth before. I didn't question it, as it slowly, steadily grew stronger.

A powerful presence had entered Zaeden's room. The knowledge that I was being gifted with peace and strength was undeniable and I welcomed the gifts as they settled assuredly within me.

I looked around the hospital room with a new awareness of our situation. I sensed that a blessing was being showered on our family, right then and there, with Zaeden lying in the midst of all that love.

My thoughts reversed course. Instead of the lonely, forsaken, deep inward spiral, I felt myself spiraling externally and drawing those around me into a protective, peace-filled hug. A sadness pained me, but it was not my own. It was the sadness of the others in the room. I felt their sadness drawing into myself, taking it from them.

As that sadness swirled through me, I gained a clearer understanding of their perspectives. This was their brother that had always been a bright spot in their day. It didn't matter what time of day or evening they arrived home, he always greeted them with a smile and said, "You're home! You're home!"

This was their baby brother, whom they had been so scared for when he was an infant, because doctors had discovered an accumulation of benign fluid between his skull and brain. He had a shunt inserted that drained the fluid out. He had a full, quick recovery, and was immediately alert with a playful personality.

Since then, we'd all been even more protective of him. We carried him, not wanting him to fall or bump himself. But he was an energetic, happy little boy who loved life. He loved learning, and often put his hands to the side of our face when we carried him and turned our head to make us look at whatever he wanted to know more about.

As we carried Zaeden from room to room, we all learned his favorite thing to do. He was absolutely amazed and thrilled when he looked out a window and saw birds flying through the air. "Birdie! Birdie!" he would say with pure delight. He stared at them, and wiggled as we held him, and wanted to go outside to be with the birdies. He watched where they flew, where they landed, how many there were, and what colors they were.

One of the ways we could get Zaeden to sleep at night was to take him to the window and let him see that it was dark. We'd tell him that the birdies were sleeping, and that he needed to sleep, too. He understood that, but as soon as it got light outside, he woke up and wanted to look at the birdies through the windows again. I often wondered why he had such a fascination with watching birds.

I'd closely monitored him after his surgery, comparing his growth and development to our other children's progress. Month  after month, I was reassured and relieved. He was doing fine. Subsequent doctor visits confirmed that, as well.

In fact, he was proving how smart he was. With so much attention paid to him by each of us, he could have become spoiled. Instead, he used the attention to learn about everything around him.

In the morning, with the sunlight in the windows, he'd want to get up, but I'd try to snuggle a quilt around him in the hope he'd lay still for another five minutes. My grandma had made that quilt many years ago. It had rows of brightly colored blocks of cloth sewed together, and then tied to a light blue cloth backing. He'd lie beside me and raise the quilt up in the air, holding it up between him and the window. The quilt had a stained glass effect being held up to the sunlight, and the colors were fascinating to him. He'd point to a block through the backside of the quilt and enthusiastically name the colors. Soon, I couldn't help but be wide-awake and smiling, with him nestled so close to me in sheer delight at the bright colors of a new day. What a beautiful way to start the morning!

With ten children, Jim and I tried to juggle the kids' needs, our jobs, the chores at home and the farm, and whatever else came up. Along the way, the kids each learned to change diapers, fix bottles, and care for a sibling. When one of the older kids required our time and attention, we often assigned one of the

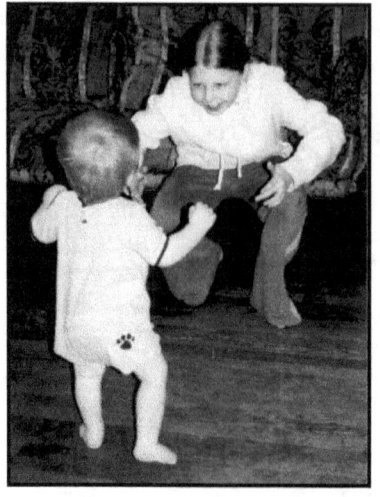

other kids to directly care for Zaeden and Macrae. We'd say, "Kael, you've got Zaeden; Grace, you've got Macrae." It was

awesome to come into a room with Chandler reading a book to Macrae, or Adriel and the little guys sitting on the floor, with Legos or various boxed food items under construction all around them.

When I came home from work, Zaeden would hear me and come running to me. "You're home. Mommy, you're home!" He'd express that excitement in seeing me with his whole body. I'd scoop him up and he'd give me one of his famous "Zaedy Bear" hugs. He'd grab around my neck with his little arms and get every

bit of his body around mine. He'd be grabbing me so tight that his whole body would be shaking. What a welcome home! Every time.

Again and again, we were blessed with his childish joy at life. We adored him and he adored each of us. The older kids each had so much opportunity to play with and care for their littlest siblings – Blaes, Macrae, and Zaeden. Jim and I understood when they would be quick with a "Why can't someone else watch them?" But, the kids all knew that we were blessed with having the little ones, and even when they wanted to do other things, they were okay with watching them instead. We were all so thankful to have Zaeden in our family.

And so, as we all stood around his bed, watching him fight for his life, not one of us was ready for him to leave us. Not one of us even knew quite what to say, but our hearts were overflowing with love and grief. And God was there among us.

# Gratitude

God had calmed me. He gave me peace and now guided me to a plan to help my family. I remembered a family tradition. For as long as the kids could remember, our Thanksgiving dinner had included sitting around the table with

glasses of sparkling apple cider or sparkling grape juice. One by one, we'd say what we were thankful for. Perhaps one child was thankful for the Thanksgiving meal, another for good grades, and another for pumpkin pie or new shoes. I was always thankful for the same thing each year, and all the kids knew it by heart. I was thankful that we could all be together. And that truly was all I ever wanted. That was at the heart of what Thanksgiving meant to me.

So, it seemed appropriate that we should now have a special Thanksgiving for Zaeden. When I suggested that we do that, the kids all seemed to realize that Zaeden wouldn't be with us for Thanksgiving anymore. The look of pain and anguish was horrible to watch, but I knew that if we could get through this, it would be a meaningful tribute to Zaeden and a wonderful memory for the rest of our family.

Each of the kids took a good amount of thought before saying what they were most thankful for about Zaeden. From oldest to youngest they took turns, and I knew it was tough, but it was also such a good, solid affirmation of how much we truly were thankful to have him in our family.

The older kids all found something wonderful to say that brought us great memories of him – thankful that he gave great hugs, thankful that he loved colors and wanted to play with a basketball, thankful that he had such curiosity and big blue eyes, etc. However, it took us by surprise and shifted our focus when Blaes, being only seven years old, simply said, "I'm thankful Zaeden gets to go to a better place."

Wow! Out of the mouths of babes. Yes, that was what we needed to be thankful for. Not for how much he had meant to us and how wonderful our lives had been with him. Zaeden was going home to Jesus, and Blaes sincerely was thankful for that.

Macrae, our three year old, didn't understand what we were talking about, and all of the monitors and tubing in and around Zaeden scared him. But, as Jim held him, with the rough and tumble playfulness that he's always had, Macrae gave a great description of how he and Zaeden played together. And, lately, Zaeden had been getting more daring with Macrae. He would run to him and lie on top of him and grab hold of him, just playing. But, Macrae knew better than to do anything to hurt Zaeden, so he'd just let Zaeden be feisty. The two of them would roll around and laugh, and we saw that they enjoyed being brothers. So, now Macrae pinched his own cheeks and roared, "RRRrrr, that's what Zaeden does!" and then tugged at his own hair like Zaeden would be pulling it and said, "Ouch!" even though we all knew that Macrae and Zaeden would never hurt each other, ever. Macrae brought laughter into that hospital room, bless his heart.

Jim said he was thankful that he had such a loving son as Zaeden. I was next, and they knew what I would say. And I said it. And meant it. I was thankful that for one last time, we could all be together. But, then I took the opportunity to talk about his body not being able to be with us much longer, but that his spirit would always be with us. Always. And God and Jesus would love him and take such good care of him. And that Heaven is a wonderful place, just like Blaes had said – a better place.

As we looked at Zaeden, we couldn't deny that he needed to go to Heaven. We didn't want him to live the way he was in that hospital bed. That would be selfish. And that would not be how Zaeden wanted to live. We all knew that in our hearts.

We then said the same prayer our family has said at night forever.

*"Now I lay me down to sleep,*
*I pray the Lord our souls to keep.*
*If we should die before we wake,*
*I pray the Lord our souls to take. Amen."*

And then, of course, the Lord's Prayer.

*"Our Father, who art in Heaven,*
*Hallowed be Thy name.*
*Thy kingdom come,*
*Thy will be done, on earth as it is in Heaven.*
*Give us this day our daily bread.*
*And forgive us our trespasses,*
*as we forgive those who trespass against us.*
*And lead us not into temptation,*
*but deliver us from evil.*
*For Thine is the kingdom,*
*and the power, and the glory,*
*forever and ever. Amen."*

Those prayers had extra-special meaning as the words worked their way through us. Knowing that God was in Zaeden's room listening to our prayers provided peace, comfort, and some healing of our pain. I sensed that our family was ready to let God help us take the next step forward.

As I looked at my family gathered around Zaeden, the connection with God was so apparent that I completely let go of all my pain and anger. I realized that He had come to me, but only because I had chosen to let Him in. I pondered the wonder of it all. I knew that God was with me, all through me, and all around me. For the first time, I sensed with keen awareness the truth and beauty of Heaven, and the delight of a spiritual world that does not have pain, or anger, or loneliness. I understood that I was being given many blessings right then and there – of strength to get through this tragedy, of wisdom to act and speak to help my family get through this, and peace to calmly lead the way and help each of them be open to receive God, as well.

I had never, ever felt so serene. I knew that we were all going to get through this together. And I was so thankful, yet so humbled, to have received such a blessing from God.

# Love Connection

Jim and I decided it was important to offer each of the kids time to be alone with Zaeden. Taralyn generously offered to wait until last, so Schuyler, our 20-year-old son, walked down the hall with me to Zaeden's room. Schuyler quietly said he would prefer to talk with Zaeden alone, so I said that I'd be right outside the door. Oh, that was tough! I realized that even though he was an adult and in college, he truly loved his baby brother. He was in with Zaeden for what seemed the longest time, but we'd agreed that the kids could

have as much time as they wanted. Sandy and I talked outside the hospital room, waiting for Schuyler, and she caught a glimpse of his anguish. I saw that reflected in her expression. But, neither of us disturbed his time with Zaeden. He looked of sorrowed exhaustion as he left Zaeden, and I walked him back to the waiting room. Our hearts were hurting, but no words were needed.

I was thankful that the previous week had been college spring break and that Schuyler and Taralyn had both been home the entire week. Schuyler was busy working several days to earn car payment money, but he had spent a good amount of time playing with his siblings. Now, that time spent with Zaeden had escalated to precious, filled with fresh, priceless memories of happiness.

●●●

As I walked toward Zaeden's room with Nolan, I thought of how much Zaeden had truly adored him. So many of Zaeden's evenings were spent on a bleacher in a gymnasium watching his big brother playing basketball. From the time Zaeden was only a little past one year old, he was trying to bounce a basketball in our living room after he'd see Nolan play ball. His most famous phrase this past winter was "Nolan, shoot the ball!"

Zaeden insisted on wearing an orange and black Tigger sweater with ears on the hood and Nolan could easily see him cheering in the stands. When he got squirmy during a basketball game, there was always a friend of the family who would be anxious to play with him, feed him popcorn, or just cuddle with him. 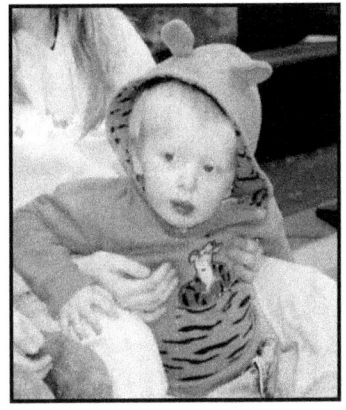 Zaeden also knew Nolan's teammates, who would also look up and smile when they heard Zaeden cheering for them.

Now, walking down the hallway to Zaeden's hospital room, I remembered that we had been at Nolan's winter sports banquet when Zaeden choked on the fruit. It's not easy to see an 18-year-old grieve over his two-year-old brother. Nolan quietly said that he would rather have time alone with Zaeden, and I knew it would be good for the two of them to do that. As I knelt outside the waiting room, I sensed incredible pain inside Zaeden's room. I peeked in, seeing Nolan, at 6'3" bending lovingly over Zaeden and having such a tough time. It was a long time before he was ready to walk back to the waiting room.

•••

As Chandler and I headed toward Zaeden's room, I remembered his easy-going nature when he was with the little guys. Blaes, Macrae, and Zaeden all looked up to him, and I often knew exactly where they were by the sound of little basketballs bouncing accompanied by giggling. Even though I'd told them time and again to roll balls in the house, I'd always had to say it with a smile. I knew better, and so did they. Basketballs were meant to be shot, not rolled! When they weren't shooting a ball

around, they were reading, or playing on the floor, or watching TV, or building blocks. Chandler was always happy to have the little guys around him.

After a few minutes of Chandler being in Zaeden's room, I realized that even though he had wanted to spend time alone with him, at only 15 years of age it was way too difficult. My heart bled for him. It was so incredibly hard to bear looking at the two of them. As I walked slowly toward him, I noticed that he was tenderly holding Zaeden's hand. How could he say goodbye to his baby brother that he's loved so much? I ached with a need to help him through that. I had no idea what to do or say, but I knew that God did. *Oh dear Heavenly Father, please help me to help Chandler.* I wanted to be the vessel through which He could pour out comfort to my children.

As I looked at Chandler and Zaeden, my focus rested on their hands clasped together. I felt the love in my heart pulsing throughout me. I remembered the special connection of how love magically flows between two people as they hold each other's hands.

I sat on the bed beside Chandler, and held his hand with Zaeden's. We talked for a little while and then I asked him if he could feel Zaeden's love through their holding hands. He said, yes, that he could, and I told him I was going to do something amazing.

I took my hand from on top of their hands and traced my finger from Chandler's hand up his arm. I asked him if he could feel that and I explained that that was Zaeden's love going up his arm. I kept tracing my finger up his arm to his shoulder and across his chest, and I asked him if he knew where that love was going. He guessed. Yes, he was right. I explained that Zaeden's love was flowing straight into Chandler's heart.

When I got to Chandler's heart, I pressed my palm against it and pressed in, asking Chandler if he could feel that love now fill his heart. Chandler looked so thoughtful and peace-filled and I knew God had provided a simple, but powerful connection for them. I then took my finger and traced up Zaeden's arm and to his heart, explaining to Chandler that his love was filling Zaeden's heart. The beauty of love flowing through all of us was so tangible, and so awesome.

After a time, I took Chandler's hand and moved it away from Zaeden's. Looking at him, I asked if, even though Zaeden's hand was no longer being held by his, if he could still feel Zaeden's love in his heart. He smiled a peaceful, content smile and said, "Yes." I explained that their love would always be in each other's hearts, no matter what happened and that even death would not separate our love for each other.

After Chandler and I talked some more about how close he felt to Zaeden and how difficult this was, I realized that I needed something to help them be okay with what death means. *Guide me again, Lord. How do I explain death to them?*

The only other deaths the kids knew about were my grandmother's death almost ten years ago and Jim's mom's death three years ago. When my grandmother died we were living in Germany, and Jim and the kids weren't able to fly back for the funeral. Our family had travelled to Jim's mom's funeral in North Dakota. Both funerals had been somber and stoic, adhering to the traditional liturgy of a Christian burial service. The kids did not know their grandparents very well. Our family's work and school schedules hadn't seemed to allow us to visit them more than twice a year. *Oh Lord, the kids loved their grandparents, but this death is so different. Please, please help us.*

A conversation that I'd had with Taralyn earlier that evening came to mind. She had been so upset, saying that she regretted spending the previous fall college semester in Australia because now she'd rather have spent that time with Zaeden and the kids. When she had first approached Jim and me with the idea of going with a group of her college friends for a college-arranged semester abroad in Australia, I was nervous about allowing her to go, but we encouraged her, saying that it would be the opportunity of a lifetime. The kids were all sad that Taralyn would be gone for the entire semester, because she often came home from college for weekends and summers to spend time with them. She has always been the ultimate big sister, getting them to clean house, playing with them, cuddling them to sleep at naptime, and has been my right hand in helping raise them. She promised to buy them each a souvenir and that they could talk to each other by using the computer.

It occurred to me as I recalled those memories, that we shouldn't tell Zaeden "goodbye." I pondered the concept of death, and understood that it is merely a separation of a spirit from a physical body into God's Heavenly presence. I hadn't understood that in its simplicity before, and was caught off-guard. I asked Chandler if we could think about Zaeden going to Heaven being the same as when we had a going away celebration for Taralyn going to Australia. Chandler agreed, and it seemed to both of us that "vacation" was a good term to use with death. Yes, we should not be saying "Goodbye," but rather, "See you, later."

I recalled with Chandler that when Taralyn had left in July for Australia, December seemed far away. Yet, in mid-December, when the kids and I met Taralyn at the airport, the time we'd been apart seemed to have magically compressed into only a short while. How strange; yet it seemed so natural.

What a great concept to apply now, using "vacation" and "see you, later" when we talked with Zaeden. Those words had comfort and reassurance and meaning that connected us with a recent family event. I was thankful that Taralyn's strong love for the kids could now help them understand that love is not connected with time.

A quiet calm settled in amongst Chandler and Zaeden and me. We were still very sad, but it was understandable to us, finally. Death no longer had control over our love connection. I thanked God, over and over, and then I thanked Chandler for being so loving to Zaeden. I assured him that God would help us all through this sad time.

•••

As a 7$^{th}$ grader, Kael was showing great logical ability and a passion for science. A year ago, he'd entered an essay contest and was one of two kids awarded a free week at Space Camp in Huntsville, Alabama. He has preferred to draw complex pencil designs of sports coliseums, monsters with mega-weaponry, and 3D architectures. Kael and Zaeden shared a passion for engineering Lego contraptions. He was patient, teaching Zaeden to say words clearly, and being specific with colors and animal names. Zaeden thrived on the seriousness of their times together.

Zaeden loved being taught anything – anything at all. His curious little face with those huge blue eyes drew all the kids to him.

For as much as Kael is a logical, serious kid through and through, I wondered how well he could cope with this emotional distress. The pain in his eyes confirmed that he was struggling with the not-so-logical connections of caring and love he shared with Zaeden. Grief is not logical.

As Kael and I sat with Zaeden, I noticed him holding Zaeden's left hand. I repeated the handholding and tracing explanation and yes, Kael said he felt Zaeden in his heart. I was relieved, because that was what all of us needed to rely on at this point. Kael smiled and simply accepted that awesome love sharing, and didn't seem to need a logical explanation for feeling that love and peace.

Kael and I talked about Taralyn's "vacation" and how it would probably be a lot of years before any of us got to be in Heaven, too. I suddenly realized the logic of something very profound. The Bible says that God is always with us and Jesus is always with us, and that God and Jesus are in Heaven. Then… why yes, it seems logical that Heaven is with us, as well. Heaven must be near to us, perhaps we just can't see clearly into that spiritual dimension during our life here on earth! Why hadn't I ever comprehended that before?

Perhaps our logic is so strongly connected with our brain, that we think we need to analyze everything to understand it. However, we all know that our human brain is limited and cannot comprehend something as profound as God and Jesus and the Holy Spirit and Heaven, let alone our spirit in relation to all of that. Wow. I realized then that my tracing of love from Zaeden to each child and from each child to Zaeden was a way to say that our spirit, our souls, are connected to him.

How appropriate that the connection of our love is in our hearts, because that has long been the symbol for our soul. Zaeden's love could not be connected to our brain, because that is just a part of our earthly body. Our heart, too, is a part of our earthly body, but it represents our spirit. It is physically central to our being, just as our spirit is the core of our existence.

I got it. I understood that gift from God. And I understood how important it was to have each of the kids receive that gift from Zaeden in a physical way so that their brain could accept what they knew in their heart.

As Kael and I walked back to the waiting room, I apologized to him because I needed him to lead the way. With all the curves and paths in the floor design of Children's Hospital, and probably due to the circumstances, I was disoriented, and didn't remember which way to go to the waiting room. Kael smiled, and of course, led the way back. He and I both knew that I was not logically strong-minded.

•••

My heart so ached for the special burden that Adriel and I shared with Zaeden. She had been with him and first noticed him choking on the fruit. She had told Grace to call me to come help and then she'd run while carrying Zaeden to get help from a neighbor. Such responsibility. Such maturity. And I knew that she had also tried to get him to stop choking, and hadn't been able to get the fruit out. I knew what hell I'd already been through with my guilt and shame and feeling forsaken by God. I so wanted to protect her from that. Sandy told us that the hospital chaplain had been with our family from the first night, and had reassured all of them that this was an accident. Absolutely no one was to blame.

Adriel has been such a little mother all of her years with Blaes, Macrae, and Zaeden. She nurtured them, she taught them, she reprimanded them, and she made sure they found their favorite toy when it was lost. She fed them, she gave them baths, and she picked out matching clothes for them. Basically, whatever needed doing, she would matter-of-factly just do it. She is so like Taralyn, helping out with what needed to be done, and although she would be having her 11$^{th}$ birthday in a little over a week, she was well matured beyond that age.

As Adriel and I walked into Zaeden's room, I saw how solemn she was. She, too, had that special bond of nurturing and watching a life grow because of love and caring. And what do you do when you can no longer nurture the child that you have so loved?

I placed her hand in his left hand. That helped. We talked to Zaeden in soft voices, telling him how much we loved him. I traced the love between both of their hearts. We talked about Taralyn's "vacation" and how Heaven is all around us. She asked,

"What will happen when Zaeden dies?" and "How will his spirit go to Heaven?"

We talked a bit about that, but neither of us knew what it would be like. I was thankful that we had that time talking with him and telling him how much we loved him.

Adriel spoke loving, kind, happy words to him, but I could tell it was alongside a sadness that was hard to bear. I told her how proud I was of her and how she had done the right thing by calling me to come help. I told her I could run home faster than 911 could've gotten dispatched and that his best chance at survival was because I had been there so quickly, even having the miracle of someone driving me partway home. She reminded me that she had recently learned the Heimlich maneuver in school and had even seen a TV show just a couple days before explaining it, too. In tears, she whispered to me that she was so sorry she hadn't gotten the fruit out when he was first choking. I assured her she had done all the right things by trying the Heimlich maneuver and hitting him on the back to try to get the fruit out, but even I hadn't been able to get it out. There was no blame to be had with this. None.

A special bond of love and peace and comfort flowed amongst Zaeden, and Adriel, and me. *Heavenly Father, thanks for letting the three of us share this special time together.*

•••

Grace and I had our time with Zaeden next. Grace and Adriel are my springtime babies, born just 13 months apart and soon to be 10 and 11 years old. How time marches forward. I remembered that Grace had sung in church just a month or so ago. She was named for my grandmother, Grace Wallman.

As Grace and I sat with Zaeden, I could see that she was experiencing a mix of emotions. She carefully sat by Zaeden, and her love for him was strong and clear. She cried a little, but then allowed God to move her spirit as she sang in a sweet, strong, but sad voice the words and sign language to "Jesus Loves You."

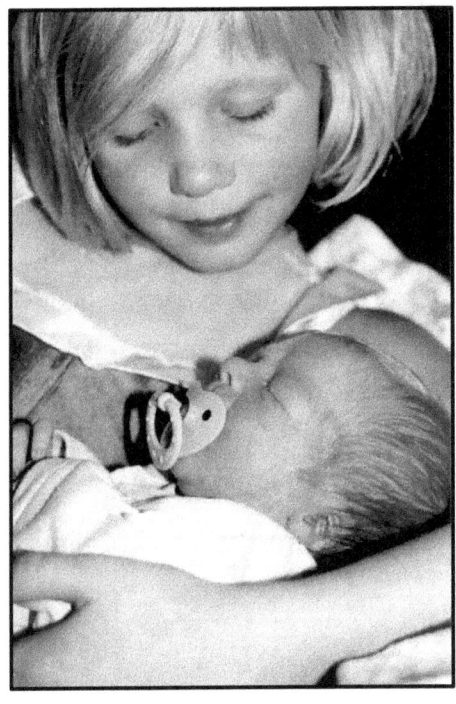

What a powerful testimony to the ease and simplicity with which children understand life and faith and love for each other and God and Jesus. Grace was giving Zaeden the most precious gift she could, that of her voice singing assurance to him that Jesus loved him and would always take care of him. I was so proud of her and so thankful that she had the courage to give such a wonderful gift, even in her grief.

I talked with Grace a bit, and we did the hand tracing and talked about the vacation that Zaeden would have with Jesus. She seemed tired, but realized the importance of what we were doing and talking about. She said she felt Zaeden's love deep in her heart. What a beautiful experience!

•••

By this time, it was getting late into the night, well after 2:00 a.m. Blaes, only seven, and I were both tired, but even more sad.

Blaes had always been a logical, sweet, considerate child, and it was heartbreaking to see him so sad.

I told him how proud I was of him, and that I knew Zaeden and he loved each other so much, and what an awesome big brother he was to both Macrae and Zaeden.

Blaes touched him and talked to him. As they held hands I did the magical tracing of Zaeden's love to Blaes' heart, and at the same time I traced Blaes' love to Zaeden's heart. Blaes smiled then, a genuine "I

got it, Mom!" smile. He said that yes, he did have Zaeden's love in his heart and could feel it strongly after I had "crawled" it all the way up his arm and over to his heart. Such blessed peace shone from Blaes' smile. Such blessed assurance that God would not sever the love between these children, ever.

• • •

Jim and I both knew that Macrae had a tough time earlier that evening because Zaeden was not awake, and because he was hooked up to all the monitors and tubing. Macrae had been confused by that, and was upset that Zaeden had to be like that. He kept telling us that Zaeden was sick, and burying his head into Jim's shoulder like he couldn't bear to see him like that.

I couldn't blame him. It didn't seem right at all for our baby to be so sick that he couldn't wake up. Macrae didn't want to stay long with him, but he did look at Zaeden from Jim's arms, with his head resting sadly on Jim's shoulder.

We told him that Zaeden was going on vacation with Jesus to Heaven. He listened intently, and looked sad, but it seemed that he somewhat understood that his best friend, his little playmate, his baby brother was going to Heaven.

Jim asked Macrae if he remembered how much fun he, Blaes,  and Zaeden had when swimming every day on our family vacation to Florida last summer. Macrae smiled a huge smile and reached out to touch Zaeden lovingly on his hand. I had long thought that children understand truths and concepts better than adults. Now I fully believed it.

•••

 Taralyn had wanted to be last and she'd waited patiently all this time. It was close to 3:00 a.m. She wanted to be alone with him and I understood how important that was.

When she came home from college early on Friday afternoons, she'd often go to the sitter and pick up the little guys.

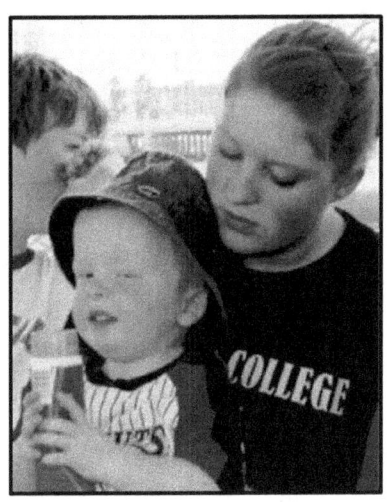

She couldn't stand to be without them if they were able to be with her. She would stop by our office with them so that we could see them, too, and then walk home with them, and read to them, and play with them.

One of her favorite things to do was to take a nap with them lying close to her. She said that Zaeden would just lie on her chest and in no time he would be so relaxed he'd just fall asleep. She loved all of the kids deeply and completely. I knew this was hard for her. I was so proud of her, though, because she had been so strong and patient and caring to all of them while we had been in the hospital with Zaeden.

Before I left them alone, I traced their love to each other's hearts, and then told her how wonderful a gift it was to all of them that she had been on "vacation." It's strange how sometimes something that had seemed so difficult all of a sudden has such great, positive meaning. I told her that I'd talked with each of the kids about her "vacation" to Australia being so similar to Zaeden being able to be on vacation with Jesus in Heaven.

Taralyn's expression conveyed thought-filled wonder mixed with gratitude as she realized the tremendous gift she had unknowingly given our family. I sensed comfort and peace settling into not only her, but Zaeden as well.

While Taralyn shared some alone time with Zaeden, I went back to the waiting room to get Schuyler and Nolan. I realized while I was with her that the tracing of love and the vacation discussions had started when Chandler had been with Zaeden. I spoke separately with Schuyler and Nolan. Each of them accepted the wonder and truth of having Zaeden's love forever in their hearts, and agreed that using "vacation" in context of eternal life with Jesus was a good analogy. We all sat together in silence then, exhausted with grief, but solid in the knowledge that love transcends all else in this world.

# Saying Goodbye

It was well past 3:00 a.m. when Taralyn came out of Zaeden's room, and amazingly six hours had passed since the doctor had told us that Zaeden was failing. He had, however, been stable the entire time that the kids had been with him. Jim and I were so thankful for that, and we settled all of the kids in the waiting room, telling them to relax and go to sleep. We assured them that if anything changed we would wake them. They were all exhausted, and soon relaxed into sleep.

Jim and I walked back to Zaeden's room and were alarmed to find several nurses at his side. I looked at the monitor and was frightened to see his blood pressure at 24/18. I couldn't believe it.

He had been stable just minutes before.

The doctor gave orders for medication to raise his blood pressure, and then to give more, and more again. The staff administered the medication through his IV and slowly his blood pressure began to rise. The doctor explained that this was part of the neurological deterioration process. If Zaeden's blood pressure couldn't be regulated it would be devastating. His heart was already having a difficult time distributing the blood appropriately, and not having good blood pressure would limit the blood flow even more.

She explained that there was a maximum that they could give him, and if his blood pressure didn't stabilize and his heart couldn't pump the blood as needed, the ventilator wouldn't be of any help. I had not understood the process before then. Jim and I stood there, holding hands tightly in silent prayer, hoping that his blood pressure would continue to rise toward normal. It did. We sat near him, holding his hands within ours, and cried and prayed and continued to shower him with our love.

My sisters and a couple of others had come into Zaeden's room, and we all realized the critical state of his beautiful, young life. With relief, we saw that his blood pressure stabilized again, and realized that we were given another gift of time to be with him. We talked and shared our concerns, and I spoke with them about the tracings and "vacation" discussions I'd had with the kids. It was a wonderful time for us to share with him.

About 20 minutes later, however, his blood pressure dropped again and the nurses quickly administered yet more medication. They reached just below the maximum medication before Zaeden responded and his blood pressure again read 120. I realized that if it dropped again, we would probably reach the maximum and his death could be just minutes after that.

Jim and I agreed that we needed to wake the kids to be with Zaeden. We'd promised to wake them if his condition changed. As they awoke with difficulty from their sleep, we relayed Zaeden's serious condition. Scooping the little ones into our arms and with the older kids steadying the younger ones, we all hurried to be with Zaeden. As we gathered around Zaeden, several of the kids began crying, and soon the grief had engulfed each of us. I saw that the kids were trying to be brave, but that they were also extremely frightened, having been woken out of sound sleep. *Oh dearest God, please not now, please not like this.*

I was too exhausted to even think, but swallowed hard to steady my breathing, and simply started voicing our nighttime prayers. As if in automatic mode, the kids became attentive and we all grasped hands, now reciting the words of truth in unison. As the words flowed steadily and with sure voicing, we were all reminded that God was not only listening but was right there in the midst of us. At Amen, the solemn understanding that God would take care of all of us held us in reverent silence. We remembered again that no matter what, Zaeden was in God's care.

I calmly explained to them how important it was for his blood pressure to remain steady. None of us knew what would happen next or how we would get through it. It was so difficult to see him lying there; us so focused on the numbers displayed by the monitors, knowing how close he was to death. But, we knew that we needed to be there with him.

All of us stood completely still, gathered closely near Zaeden. Our eyes focused first on Zaeden, then on the blood pressure monitor, then back to Zaeden. We saw normal readings of 120, then 119, then 121, then 118, then 122. Ten minutes later it was still stable. Fifteen minutes later it was still stable. Twenty minutes later it was still stable. The scared feeling settled into a comfortable acceptance. I noticed that all of the friends and family who had been sleeping in the waiting room had now gathered around us to be with Zaeden. The shared love with all of us together in his room completely filled those walls to overflowing.

He was still breathing harsh breaths periodically, and we all listened and watched, with our hearts breaking, but pouring out love for him. As the half hour mark went by, I realized that his love for us matched ours for him. He desperately clung to life for us. We cried as silently as possible, and said quiet prayers, and shared hugs and words of comfort to each other and to him.

Still his blood pressure remained stable. It grew more quiet and calm in the room. The nurses brought blankets and pillows for each of us. One by one, each of the kids and the others in the room settled in to sleep. Jim slept with Macrae in his arms. Taralyn held Blaes close to her. Julee and I remained at Zaeden's side, across the bed from each other. I saw that she was praying and trying to stay awake. I vowed that I would not leave his side and I touched his leg to let him know that I was there even when I wasn't speaking to him. I lay my head down by his leg and cried. I didn't want my baby to die, but knew that God already had Zaeden cradled in His arms, ready for the time when he would be going to Heaven.

I watched the monitor even as everyone else slept, continuing the vigil of prayer and wakefulness. I looked around the room, and realized how wonderful it was that Zaeden could be surrounded by this awesome love. I simultaneously thanked God that Zaeden had so awesomely loved each of us. How could it be that such a little guy could have so much love for each and every one of us?

The night was still deep in darkness. I remembered Zaeden often waking in the darkest of night and crying out. After his surgery, Jim or I always comforted him in the night. If he'd fallen asleep in his bunk bed and then woken up scared, we'd calm him and then bring him into our bed. After a few minutes of tossing and turning and cuddling and wiggling, he'd settle again into deep sleep. I never, ever regretted waking up at night to comfort him.

In the darkness of that Thursday night, I caressed Zaeden, like so many nights before. I was so tired, beyond exhaustion, but I wanted to stay awake. I begged God to please not let Zaeden die in the darkness of night, but instead to keep Zaeden alive so that when he went to Heaven it would be light and he could see the birdies. *Please, God...*

I heard the hospital room door sliding open and saw the doctor coming toward me. It was light outside, and I quickly looked at my watch. 6:00 a.m.! I had fallen asleep. Frantically, I looked at Zaeden. He was still pink and the ventilator still worked steadily. Blinking hard to steady my focus, I looked at the monitor and with immense relief I noted that the blood pressure numbers were still normal and stable.

The doctor beckoned me into the hallway. She looked so sad and tired from the anxious watchfulness of the night. She explained with genuine sorrow that she and the staff had been watching all of our family so peacefully sleeping and lovingly surrounding Zaeden in the darkest of the night. She said that Zaeden must have known that he was so cared for and loved, and had waited until we were all asleep for him to take his last breath on his own. The ventilator was the only thing keeping him alive now.

She explained that his blood pressure and heart rate were stable, but that because he was no longer breathing on his own, complete brain death had probably occurred. The testing for that needed to be done twice and would be tested by taking the ventilator out and seeing if he could breathe on his own over a period of several minutes. She stated that over the past hour or so they had been watching the monitors for signs of spontaneous breathing, but there had been none. Zaeden's basic connection with life, even at a survivalist level, was gone.

Numbly, I walked back into Zaeden's room. The light of a beautiful sunny day was streaming through his windows. I thanked God that He had given us until morning. Another blessed miracle.

I awakened Jim and my sisters and told them of Zaeden's status. We calmly woke the kids and told them they could each spend time with Zaeden again that morning. After checking on Zaeden to be sure that he was really still stable, they went to the waiting room to stretch and fully wake up from the challenges of the night before.

Jim and I watched from Zaeden's bedside as the hospital staff performed the testing. It was awful and agonizing to see him not breathe at all over the course of those minutes. We fully realized then that his brain functionality was completely gone. At the same time, I knew, I could fully sense, him being still there in spirit in his physical form.

Zaeden looked so much more peaceful when they were doing the testing, without the ventilator. It simply seemed wrong to keep him attached to such a constrained life, when he had been so bright and full of life just days ago. The doctor said that a neurologist would need to repeat the testing in an hour or so. She explained that if that test had the same results, the ventilator would need to be removed soon afterward.

I knew that an hour would not be enough time for each of the kids to spend time with him again before the second test was repeated, so I told her that we would not allow them to remove the ventilator until each of the kids had time to be with him again.

While Jim took the kids to the cafeteria for breakfast, my sisters and I waited with Zaeden. I thought about the handprints we had tried to do the day before. We'd asked the hospital staff if they had any paint and paper to do a handprint and footprint of Zaeden. They had found some, and one of the nurses helped us. Only a couple of handprints had turned out well and we'd initially thought that we'd make copies for each of the kids as a keepsake. Now I realized that it would be better if each of the kids had a real painted handprint, instead of just a copy. We had used Zaeden's left hand for the handprint, the hand that we had traced his love from during the night. That would be a wonderful gift to give the kids to remind each of them of the tracing of love to their hearts.

We asked one of the nurses if they could find the same paint and more paper for us. In a matter of minutes, they brought it in, and Jim, Taralyn, Julee, and I carefully painted his hand the many times it took to get enough handprints for each of the kids and also for Greg, Sandy, and Julee. The paint just happened to be blue, his favorite color. I saw in the handprints such a bright reminder of the liveliness in his big, blue eyes.

We finished the handprints and set them to dry in a line along the windowsill that ran the entire length of the room. The day was shining a bright blue sky at us through that window. It seemed strange sensation; none of us were fully awake, but we didn't seem tired either. Time seemed to be something that others were keeping track of and needing to go by. Time had no meaning to me. I only knew that I needed to be with Zaeden.

The neurologist came into the room and explained that they were there to do the second test. Jim and I steadied ourselves to go through the procedure again with Zaeden.

The results were the same. Zaeden was declared brain dead.

There was no decision to be made as to whether or not we would take him off life support. In the case of brain death, the parents had no choice; the ventilator would be removed.

I again explained that we needed time for each of our kids to spend time alone with Zaeden. I also told the staff that I wanted to be on the bed holding him and they should detach any unnecessary monitors and tubing. It seemed that the more natural we could make this last time with him, the easier and better for him and for us.

I sat on the bed and the nursing staff carefully maneuvered the tubing and monitors so that they were not as noticeable. I cradled him on my lap and treasured having his skin touching mine, completely supported by my body. Such strong physical bonding, I soaked it in as deeply as it would go, way down to the depth of my heart, my soul.

We put Zaeden's Pooh blanket lovingly around him, and his teddy bears close to him. Each of the kids patiently waited for their turn to be with Zaeden again. As I held him, they sat on the bed as near to him as they could, and talked with him, and read to him, and cried, and remembered with me so many special times with him. That second time of being able to be with him was so healing, and very powerful in the light of day. It seemed we all sensed that God was watching over us and helping us.

Calm replaced the frantic anxiety of the night. I asked each of the kids to remember the love traced to their hearts and his heart. Each of them nodded, and in deep thought instinctively reached out to touch his hand they'd held the night before. Amazing. With me holding Zaeden it seemed that treasured love went deeper and broader and somehow connected all of us. Our hearts were being broken, but yet somehow were healing because of Zaeden's love for us and our love for him.

The hospital staff gifted us with a small box of care items and sincerely offered condolences. One of the items I noticed immediately was a disposable camera. Jim and I asked Julee to take a family photo with me holding Zaeden and Jim and the kids standing around his bed. Our last family picture. I found it difficult to even look toward the camera. Raw emotion spewed out from the reality of this tragedy that we were so deeply entrenched in. There was no escaping, no prayer that a miracle of life could occur for Zaeden. Only an overwhelming sense of the last time we could be with him, his last breath, the last time we could touch him when he was alive, and the last time we would see his heart beat on the monitor.

We had already experienced so many of the lasts, but hadn't even known that they were occurring, such as his last smile, or the last time we heard his voice, or when he said his colors, or bounced a basketball, and all of the other things that we knew him to do. With a sharp intake of breath, my mind struggled to comprehend that those lasts were already only memories that would fade over time.

Time – a harsh factor of life. For the past many years, I had chased time in relentless, futile pursuit of "quality family time", "quiet time", or some other obscure escape from how complex my life had become. It had seemed important to cram as much activity and scheduling of this and that into the 24 hours of each day as our family possibly could.

Now, sitting with Zaeden cuddled on my lap, I didn't even once look at the clock, and didn't need to. There was no meaning to time at that point. Time was not going to direct my last holding Zaeden physically close to my heart. I wouldn't allow it. I would not allow the doctor to put a time limit on when we took Zaeden off the ventilator. I simply cherished holding him, touching him tenderly, and let our spirits bond as strongly as they could.

I intellectually understood that he had been declared brain dead, but even that didn't matter. His spirit was still alive in him. I could sense it being next to me so strongly. I felt it. I knew it. His spirit's presence staying close to me was undeniable. We clung together in spirit. A powerful surge of bonding occurred then, and I knew that death would never, ever separate us. I knew it. With immense relief, I realized that with our spirits there would never be a "last" anything. Our spirits were connected eternally.

When it was Adriel's turn, she sat at Zaeden's feet on the bed and was facing the window. We talked for a while, and she asked what would happen when Zaeden died. We had both questioned that during the night, but even now in the light of day we didn't know what that would be like.

I explained the basics of the physiological process, and that without the ventilator he wouldn't be getting oxygen, and then even his heart would stop. And when that happened, he would die. We talked about his going to Heaven and how Jesus would be with him. Her attention became focused on the balloons someone had given us that were on the windowsill of Zaeden's room. She thoughtfully looked at them, and then quietly asked if the kids could let the balloons go up with Zaeden when Jesus took him to Heaven. I was intrigued at her request, and pondered this very interesting idea.

I smiled and realized she had just been given a beautiful gift, a most wonderful, fun idea! I asked her to get money from Jim, and then to have Taralyn go buy enough balloons for each of the kids. She smiled a happy smile at me, and then a playful, "I've-got-a-surprise-for-you" smile at Zaeden. Jumping off the bed and carefully gathering the balloons from the windowsill, she rushed out of the room in search of Taralyn and Jim.

When my sisters found out about the idea, they thought it truly wonderful. Sandy looked out Zaeden's hospital window and tried to figure out where they could stand outside to give us the best chance to see the balloons after the kids would release them. Soon, Julee told me that the balloons were there and the kids were busy picking out their favorite one for Zaeden.

One by one, each of the kids came into the room to share special time with Zaeden. Jim and I then decided to have everyone who was in the waiting room come into Zaeden's room. I had no idea there were so many people who had come to the hospital to be with our family. By the time everybody came into Zaeden's room, it was pretty crowded, perhaps 40 of us in all. We all knew this was a last for us.

Over the course of the last few days, my family spent as much time as they could with us. My sisters, Sandy and Julee, and my brother Greg, and their spouses, and their kids had been at the hospital almost constantly. My dad and his fiancée, Donna, were there. My uncle and a cousin and his wife were there. Jim's sister Anne was there. My dear friends, Lisa and Calla, had been there. Our pastor was there as often as he could be.

Looking around the room, though, as the last few persons entered, I was shocked to discover that the majority of them were children. I hadn't known, but Jim had, that our kids' friends had been there almost the whole time. Taralyn's friends from college had been with her for the past several days. Schuyler and Nolan had several friends who had even slept in the waiting room that past night. Many younger kids were there, as well, friends of Chandler, Kael, Adriel and Grace. It was hard to believe that so many people had dropped everything to be with our family in our time of tragedy. Wow!

I didn't know how much they knew about the current situation, so I spoke to them all as I held Zaeden. I gently explained in plain words what had happened with Zaeden, what his condition was, and that the doctor had told us that he needed to have the ventilator removed. Then, with a strange sense of peace and conviction moving strongly through me as I hugged Zaeden so close to me, I shared my understanding that even though he had been declared brain dead, his spirit was still in his body and could hear us and see us. They listened intently as I explained the concept of Zaeden going on vacation with Jesus and also how Zaeden's love and spirit would always be in our hearts. The transformation was amazing to behold. The harsh pain and sorrow deeply etched in their facial expressions began to soften and lift toward hope.

Smiling softly, but speaking in deepness of love for all, I described how our family had done the tracing of Zaeden's love into each of our hearts. Smiling a big, happy smile that must have been gifted to me from deep within Zaeden, I said that even though Zaeden was such a little guy, that they all knew he certainly had more than enough love to give to each of us. As the light of smiles began to shine throughout the room, I invited each of them to have some time with Zaeden.

Pastor then said a beautiful prayer about life and eternal life and God and love. After our Amen, I noticed some persons deeply in thought, some quietly in thoughtful conversation, and some, one by one, coming near to be with Zaeden. Never had I imagined such an atmosphere of caring packed so pervasively into one hospital room. What an awesome testimonial to their strength and courage and love for Zaeden and our family. Time stood still as each person in his room, when they were ready, came to Zaeden's bed side. They hugged him, touched him, cried, and told him they loved him. They hugged me, and for each of them I traced his love to their heart.

While placing their hand into Zaeden's, I silently prayed that Jesus would grab hold of and take each person's pain and grief, and while tracing, I firmly prayed that the power of God's mercy and Zaeden's love would be placed deeply into their heart. I asked each of them if they could feel his love, and every one of them calmly and most assuredly answered yes, they could.

The story of the little boy with five fish and two loaves of bread blessed by Jesus to feed several thousand people seemed appropriately proportioned to Zaeden's love being shared amongst all of those in his room who hungered for God's answers and peace and comfort. God was powerfully amongst us, and Zaeden shared his love. For the first time, I sensed the magnitude and divine essence of spirituality moving throughout his room and the power of it connecting each one of us in love.

After a time, several of them left his room, and eventually only a few of us remained. The reality of transitioning into the next timeframe was realized. As we began quiet discussions, Taralyn said she wanted to be with Jim and me when Zaeden's ventilator was removed. Pastor would also stay with us. I knew that the balloons were ready, and Sandy said she would take the kids outside the hospital and wait with them to release the balloons. Earlier Jim had asked pastor to stay with us, and asked Lisa to be with the kids. Lisa told us that pastor would call Lisa's cell phone to let her know when to have the kids release the balloons. Lisa's expression relayed strength, love, and caring. I simply nodded in reply, entrusting her to care for our kids. As she walked out the door, I heard her call out to pastor that she was going now to be with the kids.

    It was time.

# Going Home

It was Zaeden's time to go to Heaven with Jesus. Still sitting cross-legged with Zaeden cuddled in my lap, I was so thankful to be with him. Jim and Taralyn and I stayed in Zaeden's room. Sandy and Julee and Lisa helped all the others in the waiting room group together and get ready to go outdoors and release the balloons.

The doctor came into the room and spoke to us about the procedure for removing the ventilator. I understood the process. Jim and Taralyn's expressions paled into resigned acceptance of that process. I requested that everything be removed from him, so that he could die as naturally as possible. The nurse nodded with understanding, but explained that the heart monitor needed to be in place to determine when there was no longer a heartbeat and that then he would be declared dead.

The nurses carefully and gently started removing IV lines and other monitors. It was quite a lengthy process, and I suddenly realized with alarm that my sisters and our kids and all those others that had been in the waiting room were probably standing outside waiting. Squeezing my eyes shut in prayer, I asked God to be with them and help them. Focusing again on Zaeden, the nurses and I took the time needed to lovingly unbind him from all the tubing and other monitors. The nurse shut off the heart monitor display in Zaeden's room, and said they would be watching on a monitor outside his room.

With only the heart monitor and ventilator attached, it finally seemed like Zaeden was just lying asleep on my lap. I was so comfortable with him and he just lay quietly with me, his heart beating steadily, and his cheeks pink with life. I caressed him and held him close, so close. Jim sat in a chair next to his bed and lovingly held Zaeden's hand. Taralyn sat next to him at the foot of his bed, softly caressing him. The room had become suddenly quieted. Jim and I exchanged looks, but in sadness acknowledging that neither of us knew what to say or do. With a bit of anxiety noticeably creeping in, I swallowed hard and forced it away. Looking intently at Zaeden, I felt my heart getting bigger as if being blown up like a balloon and being on the verge of bursting into brokenness. I desperately wanted Zaeden to open his eyes and look at me. I wanted to see his eyes as they would light up when he greeted me or when he learned something new. I remembered the excitement that always shined in his eyes whenever Jim or I, or any one of the kids read Zaeden's favorite books to him. Most of us had them memorized. Zaeden liked one book best. We were all sure he carried it around the house looking for yet another person, even visitors, to read it to him after one of us had just read it to him. Suddenly, I understood why he loved that book so much! Each page spoke to a vivid color. Zaeden was absolutely fascinated with colors.

Knowing that Zaeden could hear me, I said to him that I would like to read his favorite book to him. Jim met my eyes with a bit of surprise and also relief. From that I gathered a bit of strength. Enunciating each word with the attention and excitement Zaeden deserved, I pulled deep from memory each word, without having the book in hand.

**"Zaeden's Rainbow"**

*"Our family likes to play Zaeden's favorite game, 'Build a Rainbow' at our farm.*
*We each choose a color.*
*Zaeden always chooses Silver.*
*Zaeden runs to play on his Silver Swing.*
*Zaeden is ready to build the Rainbow.*
*Zaeden asks where each color is.*
*Each of us tells Zaeden where we found the color we chose.*
**'Where is Pink?'**

*'Here is Pink!'* Nolan is feeding the Pink Pig.
*'Where is Purple?'*
*'Here is Purple!'* Mom is watering a Purple Flower.
*'Where is Blue?'*
*'Here is Blue!'* Adriel is feeding the Blue Birds.
*Where is Green?'*
*'Here is Green!'* Taralyn is finding a Green Clover.
*'Where is Yellow?'*
*'Here is Yellow!'* Grace is chasing a Yellow Butterfly.
*'Where is Gold?'*
*'Here is Gold!'* Schuyler is playing with the Gold Dog.
*'Where is Brown?'*
*'Here is Brown!'* Macrae is making Brown Chocolate s'mores.
*'Where is Orange?'*
*'Here is Orange!'* Kael is watching the Orange Fish.
*'Where is Red?'*
*'Here is Red!'* Blaes is working by the Red Barn.
*'Where is Black?'*
*'Here is Black!'* Dad is feeding the Black Cow.
*'Where is White?'*
*'Here is White!'* Chandler is finding the White Eggs.
*'Where is Silver?'*
*'Here is Silver!'* Zaeden is swinging on the Silver Swing.
We build Silver and White Clouds for our Rainbow to float on.
Zaeden says, 'Hey, everybody! Look up in the sky.
Look at Zaeden's Beautiful Rainbow!'"

Instinctively I looked at Zaeden's eyes, expecting his normally excited response. Before the end of the book, Zaeden usually interrupted, either for me to read faster or to turn back to a page he wanted re-read. Zaeden's eyes did not open, though, and he lay limply in my arms. My heart beat madly and I hugged him tighter, desperately begging reality not to be. Tears began to well and spill, freely. Staring at Zaeden, the horridness of death mocked me. Zaeden's big, blue eyes would never again be able to look at the book that he so loved. I would never again be able to see him point to the pages with such excitement and ask what each of the colors was, even though he and I both knew that he had memorized all the colors.

Zaeden's body was really dying. The enormity of that realization paused my thought process. I saw then the truth, the awful truth, that the ventilator was the only reason Zaeden was alive yet. Zaeden's body could no longer keep him alive. Only a machine was helping him stay alive for a little while longer. Pursing my lips together in resolute firmness and swallowing hard to keep my breathing at a reasonable rate, I fought not to shriek and wail the bereftness that reality had stabbed me with. Closing my eyes, and looking downward, thoughts of love for Zaeden and his needs were pondered.

I did not want this. I fought the reality of his dying. My mind went into overdrive, and I imagined myself fiercely protecting Zaeden. I wouldn't let this happen. I would fight a fierce battle, refusing to let the doctor remove the ventilator. I would not let Zaeden die.

Within that imagined scene, though, I also saw the life that

Zaeden would have lying in his bed in a hospital room forever hooked up to the ventilator. In that moment of vision, I saw his life of not being able to smile at us, or speak, or look at us with excitement. I saw his life of not even being able to move any part of his body, or even to breathe by himself. I and Jim, as well as each of the kids, would not be able to be with him continuously.

The vision waged battle as I imagined joy and happiness of being able to visit Zaeden as often as I could, and be able to see his beautiful face, and caress his hands. Perhaps the nurses would allow me to help bathe him and I could lovingly towel him dry and put lotion on his so-soft skin. I wanted to do those things for him and be with him every possible moment.

Then I also envisioned me walking into Zaeden's sterile, quiet hospital room and seeing his small, frail body alone in a hospital bed. Looking around the hospital room, I saw only white walls, white blankets, white sheets, a white pillow case, blah-colored curtains and floor. Zaeden was surrounded by sterile medical devices that were forcing his body to stay alive for however long his blood pressure could remain stable.

With a sad and heavy heart, I voluntarily withdrew from the battle. I understood that Zaeden would not want that life, and we would be selfish to want that for him. His body was dying and I needed to be loving and gracious in allowing the doctors to let that to happen.

A divergent contrast formed for me then, allowing distinct separation of Zaeden's spirit from his physical body. Startled, I remembered then that his spirit was not dying. No, his spirit was still alive and would be alive even after his body was dead!

Zaeden needed to have his spirit released from his physical body so that he could again see the colors in this beautiful world. It seemed cruel to have wanted Zaeden's body to stay alive, keeping his spirit trapped inside his body that was brain-dead, lying motionless on a bed in a hospital room. I did not want that for him, or myself, or any of our family. Gazing down at his still-closed eyes, I knew he would not have wanted that either. Reality settled deep within me, and at that moment I gained an acute awareness of the truth.

The truth. Our spirits are connected in a way that our physical bodies cannot be. Our life in this earthly form is a constraint for our spirit. This physical life we lead here on earth is a process of birth and then decay. All of us will someday die. And all of us someday will have our spirit released from our body.

It doesn't matter if we are old, or young, or have physical limitations with our brain, or if our muscles are paralyzed, or if we have cancer that has invaded and destroyed our body. None of that physical aspect is important when we die. Only our spirit is important, and our spirit has nothing physical about it.

I knew then that it was Zaeden's spirit that loved us, and that was what we loved about him.

The love we felt was not just a physical love for Zaeden's body. Each one of us intensely felt and loved Zaeden's spirit. And of course, I then realized that it was not my physical being that loved Zaeden. It was my spirit that loved Zaeden's spirit. This was a new concept for me, although it seemed to make such perfect sense. It seemed that I should have realized this truth before now.

So it was that I began to look forward to Zaeden being able to have his spirit released from the brain dead body that he was trapped in. And with this anticipation, I also gained strength and happiness and peace and comfort that reached a much higher, significant level. I was truly aware of his spiritual being and the connection with my spirit. Wow!

I was ready. Jim still sat across from me at the side of the bed and Taralyn sat at the foot of the bed and held Zaeden's feet. Quietly, and tenderly, I spoke to Zaeden. I wanted to let him know what I thought would happen. I explained that soon he would probably see a bright light. My words seemed to simply flow, with serenity and happiness, affirming what I truly wanted for Zaeden, and that was for him to be able to be free to see the world again. I sensed God's calming presence and strength to let my little boy go home to Heaven. I was ready for him to go home. I was truly okay with Zaeden going to Heaven with Jesus.

I lovingly explained to Zaeden that when he saw the bright light coming toward him that it might be a little bit frightening, but that it was Jesus. And I reminded him that he knew how much Jesus loves him. I remembered Zaeden being baptized at three weeks old on my birthday, 14 November 2004. What a special birthday for me!

I remembered us bringing him to church service on Sundays, and how often we passed him from me to Jim, to Chandler, to Adriel, to Kael, etc. and then perhaps as a last resort one of us would take him to the nursery during the sermon. We didn't let him get fussy in church, because we didn't want to disrupt the service.

It was even more complicated for our family during church services because Macrae was so active. Often, we ended up passing both of them around to help quiet them or let them color on our laps, or play with my watch, or do whatever we could to keep them quiet. But Zaeden knew what going to church meant. And he knew how to pray. We prayed as a family before meals, and we held hands with those sitting next to us as we prayed.

*"God is great, God is good.*
*Let us thank Him for our food.*
*By Thy goodness, all are fed.*
*Give us Lord our daily bread. Amen."*

Because I teach Sunday School, and have for many of the past 20+ years, Jim has been the one to take the little ones to Sunday school or keep them with him during Sunday School. Macrae, being as busy as he is, has often proven challenging, and it's been no different with him in Sunday School. So, Jim would stay with Macrae during Sunday School to help, and would bring Zaeden along. Zaeden loved it. So, even though Zaeden was only two years old, he'd been going to Sunday school with Macrae this past year. And, in amongst the coloring and play dough, he'd been taught the basics of Jesus loving him and God caring for all of us.

Our church also celebrates the anniversary of baptism, and Jim and I went with Zaeden just a few months ago to that church service. Along with other parents who were celebrating their child's anniversary of baptism, we brought him to the altar to have him blessed again by pastor and to receive his baptism candle. I was so thankful that he'd experienced all of those important religious events. I knew that Zaeden knew who God and Jesus are.

*I explained it the best that I understood, and as best a mommy can to her two-year-old. It seemed pretty simple as I talked through it with him. With surprise, I suddenly realized that death is not complicated at all. It is simple. When we die, our spirit gets to meet Jesus, and we can then go with Him to Heaven.*

*After I explained to Zaeden that he would soon be seeing Jesus, and to not be afraid, I also explained that Jesus wanted him to go with Him to Heaven. I told Zaeden that I wanted him to go with Jesus to Heaven, that Heaven was a wonderful place, and that he and Jesus would be happy there. I told Zaeden that someday Jesus would come to me, and that I would go to Heaven with Jesus, and then he and I would be in Heaven together.*

*I remembered then that the kids would be outside, so I explained to Zaeden that when he was flying outside of his hospital room with Jesus, he should look outside for Schuyler, Nolan, Chandler, Kael, Adriel, Grace, Blaes and Macrae. I told Zaeden that the kids would be waiting for him outside and that they were holding balloons that they wanted to fly to Heaven with him. I told him that as soon as he and Jesus were outside the hospital that he needed to go fly to the kids and be with them as they let go of the balloons. And then he needed to fly away with the balloons to Heaven with Jesus.*

I asked Zaeden to please let the kids know that he was doing that with them. Desperately, I hoped that the kids might experience some peace or comfort somehow, because I knew that this would be so very, very difficult for them. I trusted God that somehow He would help my children through this, because I couldn't be outside to be with them now. *Please God, please God, please be with my children and help them through this. Please.*

The staff was ready. They carefully removed Zaeden from the ventilator.

Jim and Taralyn and I watched Zaeden's pink color changing to pale and then an awful ashen color as the oxygen was depleted in his body. We sat in silence watching his body die. I had no idea what to expect. I'd never been with a loved one when they died before now. I held Zaeden so very lovingly, watching intently and expectantly, for I didn't know what.

Before I was even able to think of what to do, I began singing a song to Zaeden.

As the phrases flowed softly to him, I realized how appropriate they were. It was as if I was singing the song, but hearing the words for the first time, and then realizing how beautifully, wonderfully, awesomely God provides for us in our time of need.

As the first phrases were sung however, that realization became coupled with a strange sensation, startling Jim, Taralyn, and me. Zaeden's body was going completely stiff. His hand had been relaxed in mine and his other hand in Jim's. Taralyn was sitting at his feet and holding him there. At that time, Zaeden's hand held tight to my hand and I could tell his other hand was doing the same with Jim's. His whole body was stiff and I knew something significant was occurring right then. I continued singing.

*"Jesus loves you, this I know.*
*For the Bible tells me so.*
*Little ones to Him belong.*
*They are weak, but He is strong.*
*Yes, Jesus loves you.*
*Yes, Jesus loves you.*
*Yes, Jesus loves you.*
*The Bible tells me so."*

The simplicity and pure truth of the words caught me by surprise. Although I'd known the words for about 40 years, and Grace had just sung them to Zaeden the night before, I did not ever recall them having the clear context that they did as I sang them to Zaeden.

Incredible. Yes, little ones to Him belong. Yes, they are weak, but He is strong. Yes, the Bible tells us that, and yes, Jesus loves you, Zaeden. I was completely overwhelmed by the simplicity of all this. Truly, children are so fresh from God and their spirits reflect Him so easily. What a beautiful song!

As I was singing the last lines, I felt Zaeden's body relax more and more. By the time I sang the last phrase, he was completely relaxed. Taralyn noticed a single tear that had fallen from his eye and pointed it out to Jim and me. As we all looked at Zaeden, I knew. Deep within me, an overwhelming certainty and conviction resounded.

I knew at that very moment that Zaeden's spirit had just left his body. The power of that understanding held me captive. That power seemed somehow to have penetrated all throughout me, and to be touching and surrounding me completely. It poured within me a newness and fullness of being securely embraced, compassionately cared for, and purely loved. This experience was profound, for without even thinking anything, I was given knowledge. Looking at Zaeden's body, still cradled on my lap, I realized, I knew, that it was only a shell now. His spirit was no longer trapped in his body. Looking over at Jim, I saw that he was also still in the deepness of experiencing this profound blessing. My eyes met his with mutual questioning of "What is all of this that is now happening?" Not knowing what to say, but knowing that there wasn't time for us to discuss it, I simply told him to go quickly and tell pastor that the kids should release the balloons. The doctor had not yet declared Zaeden dead, but Jim assured pastor that now was the time for them to let the balloons go.

We had been focused on Zaeden's body, but a beautiful flash of colors outside Zaeden's window abruptly caught our attention. Amazing! All of those balloons floated up into the sky in full view from the middle window of Zaeden's hospital room. I watched them slowly lift upward and out of our sight. They were a blessing – another gift from God – a reassurance that the children were being well taken care of while I was in Zaeden's room.

After the balloons flew out of sight, Taralyn turned to look at me with an expression of awe and wonder. She whispered, "Mom, what is this?" I still felt it, and now realized she had, too. The very air we breathed, and the air that touched our skin, and the lightness of the room, felt holy and serene. I looked across the bed at Jim and could see that he was experiencing the same thing. The deepness within me knew what it was. I told them we were experiencing God's presence.

The three of us sat quietly, looking at each other, feeling the power and comfort of that spiritual presence. We had no need for words. A peace that truly passes all understanding surrounded us and filled us as we quietly sat with Zaeden's body in that hospital room.

# God Is With Us

I still held Zaeden, his tubing and devices now removed, and pondered the meaning of this blessing that God had so personally gifted to us at the moment of Zaeden's death. I had now moved beyond faith in things unseen, to an absolute *knowledge* that God exists and a crystal clear certainty that He now has Zaeden spiritually alive in Heaven with Him. What a comfort!

Then another realization came to me: God is always with us, and Jesus is always with us, yet both God and Jesus are in Heaven. So, it must be true that Heaven is also with us. If Heaven is with us, then Zaeden is still with us, as well.

And if I could feel God's presence so strongly, then Zaeden's presence was also close. Zaeden was not gone. Zaeden was simply in Heaven, but was still here, still around me, so near to me it seemed he was hugging me. In that moment, I felt Zaeden's presence as a bright happiness in my heart. Zaeden's spirit was still with me!

Julee came into the room. She had been outside with the kids to release the balloons and had taken a couple of pictures of them. With a soft and caring voice, she quietly asked if I would like her to take a couple of pictures of me and Zaeden. The request seemed strange, but in my still deepness of thought I simply allowed it. Afterward, she gently sat down on Zaeden's bed to talk with us.

We told her that the balloons had floated up clearly in sight through the center of his room's window. "Did you see the silver balloon?" she asked, with a sudden hint of excitement in her voice. We hadn't.

She explained that Sandy had planned to lead the group of more than 40 people to an open area outside the hospital, where they thought the balloons could be seen from Zaeden's window. However, when they left the waiting room, she realized they wouldn't all fit into the elevator, and decided instead to lead them down a set of stairs. As Sandy reached the bottom of the stairs, she saw one doorway with a sign posted that it was only to be used in emergency. With the 40 plus number of people trailing upward behind her up the flights of stairs, she called out to our brother Greg to ask his advice. He called in reply from the top of the stairwell that she should just open it, knowing that they simply needed to get outside. Sandy opened the door and the group filed outside. As the door shut after the last person exited, Sandy realized that they were in a special fenced in outdoor area. She had led them by mistake to the hospital's helicopter landing pad. With fencing surrounding the area, and the door unable to be opened from the outside, Sandy panicked! Her college aged son, noting the distressing situation, decided to take matters into his own hands. He scaled the fence, and after calling out to get the attention of some nearby security personnel, he quickly explained their dilemma. The security personnel unlocked the door and led the group back inside the hospital. One of the security guards then graciously directed Sandy to the proper exit they could use. Sandy was by now completely stressed out, assuming that the group wouldn't have time to get outdoors again before they received the phone call to release the balloons. She called out for them to walk quickly, and silently begged God not to let Zaeden die before they could get outdoors. With a sigh of relief, they soon found themselves outdoors, exactly where she had originally planned for them to release the balloons.

Julee said then that Jim's sister Anne requested that the group form a prayer circle. Taralyn, Jim, and I listened intently as Julee explained that they had formed a prayer circle. She said that there was a strong presence of family and sharing and being together for a true purpose. As the circle was formed, no one had cared who they stood by, and it was with love and togetherness that they upheld each other and prayed the Lord's Prayer.

Standing amongst the now completely silent circle, Julee had glanced around, noticing that most of them were looking down in sadness or were crying quietly. They all realized that in a few short minutes Zaeden would no longer be alive.

However, she went on to explain, some of the people had looked up at the sky, including our dad and Donna, his fiancé. The sky was clear and sunny with a gentle breeze and something shiny had caught their attention. High above the hospital was a silver object that they first thought was an airplane. They soon noticed that it wasn't moving, and so they looked more intently at it to better see what it was. After a short time, they realized that it was a silver balloon! Dad said they had stared in awe at the shining, silvery balloon, describing how it just gently floated from side to side, as if it were tethered to the hospital.

Dad was still watching the balloon when pastor phoned Lisa to tell the kids to release the balloons. He saw with amazement that the silver balloon, still high above the hospital, began slowly floating toward the other balloons at the exact time that the kids released their balloons. All of the balloons then floated upward together.

Julee's husband Brian, and Schuyler's friend, Brandi, had also seen the silver balloon. They were astonished as well, witnessing the strange, but beautiful connection of the silver balloon to the kids' balloons.

Julee sat in silence then, as I tried to comprehend what she was relaying to us. Looking deep into her eyes, I understood that she had been profoundly moved by what they had experienced outside the hospital. God had provided yet another miracle for our family. He had gifted those outside the hospital with something that could be seen – a clear sign that Jesus was with us and Zaeden during those minutes of Zaeden dying that were so hard to bear.

Julee's smile resonated reassurance and faith, and as she reached over to hug me our tears of joy flowed freely. She further explained that when Lisa had gotten the phone call and then let them know to release the balloons, she had watched the kids slowly and sadly release their balloons. The balloons had not all been released at the same time, but separately, as each child was ready to let go.

Schuyler had been holding Macrae while everyone stood in the circle. Schuyler let go of his balloon, and one by one as the rest of the kids let go of their balloons, Schuyler tried to convince Macrae to let go of his balloon. Macrae stubbornly resisted releasing "his" balloon.

Finally Macrae realized "his" balloon was supposed to float with the other balloons and he let go, his balloon floating upward toward the already released balloons. In the silence of that sad, lovely moment when those 40 people stood looking up at the balloons floating upward, Macrae had then looked up at the balloons flying overhead and suddenly said in a happy, clear voice, "Bye, bye, Zaeden, see you!"

Immediately, there was a realization that a four-year-old's faith and Heavenly insight was all that they needed, too. Their sadness could be replaced with a certainty that Zaeden's spirit was moving through and around the group and now on his way with Jesus just above them.

Julee also said that she had felt a strong presence of God at the time when the balloons were being released. She said the feeling was something like a movement that was uplifting to her body, describing with hand motions how the movement started low on her body and lifted upward to high above her. Julee's brown eyes shined with a knowing, and a calm serenity. She was very moved by the experience, and had been comforted with the understanding that Jesus and Zaeden had truly been with them as the balloons were released.

Glancing at Jim and Taralyn I noticed that they, too, were deep in thought, attempting to comprehend the wonder and beauty of what had happened outside. Each of us sat silent and speechless, as one by one our gazes became fixed on Zaeden's body, still cradled on my lap. Within a mixture of tears and smiles, the three of us tried to put into plain words the awesome presence that we'd felt and witnessed just minutes before. As our description tumbled out, Julee's smile grew brighter. It became obvious, as the four of us nodded in sincere agreement and delight, that we had each experienced God's presence. God had truly been merciful throughout this tragic experience, but the greatest gift of all was at the moment Zaeden spiritually entered Heaven.

Pastor had come into the room while we talked with Julee. He heard us try to describe the awesome experience of Zaeden's spirit being released from his body. After he heard Julee relay their experience with the balloons, he quickly typed an email that summarized the amazing experiences. He read it to Jim and me, to make sure that he had captured it accurately, and then he sent it off to several people in the congregation.

It wasn't until then that Julee and I realized what a beautiful concert God had orchestrated for us. I had requested all of the tubing and devices be removed from Zaeden before the ventilator was removed, but that process had taken so very long. I'd become worried that the group would've been waiting for that very long time outside the hospital and had prayed to God to be with them and help them. Simultaneously, and unbeknownst to any of us in Zaeden's room, Sandy had somehow led the group outside, and inadvertently locked them into a fenced area. As the group frantically tried to make their way to the correct outdoor location, Sandy had prayed to God for help to get them outdoors before they would receive the phone call to release the balloons.

Julee and I smiled, hugged each other tightly, and cried healing tears of thanksgiving, with an even more certain knowledge that God had been watching over all of us the entire time.

Taralyn then brought the small keepsake box that the hospital staff had given us over to Zaeden's bed. We'd noticed earlier that it contained the disposable camera, but now looked to see what other items had been gifted to our family. We found a few small plastic bags and a scissors that we could use to cut off and keep some of Zaeden's hair. I remembered the haircuts that I had given the kids over the past many years. Last summer I had buzzed the little guys' hair pretty short. It was not only cute on each of them, but also great for the boys to have such short hair in the heat of an Iowa summer.

I'd noticed after the haircuts, when sweeping up the collection of hair on the kitchen floor, that Blaes had a medium brown hair, like Jim and Chandler's. Macrae had blonde hair, like Kael, Adriel, and Grace have, and like Schuyler and Nolan had when they were younger. Zaeden had the most interesting hair. We noticed shortly after his surgery that he had a wide stripe of reddish blonde hair down the center of his head. The sides and back were a much lighter reddish blonde. It made him look especially playful, and the reddish color was set off even more because of his fair complexion and big, blue eyes. He was such a beautiful child.

I hadn't had time to cut the kids' hair lately. Taralyn said that now she knew why. I carefully held Zaeden while she cut some of his hair from both the light and reddish blonde areas. We got enough to give each of the kids a bit of it, thinking that we would make a memory box for each of them. We could also include the handprints we'd made that morning. It seemed a wonderful idea, and I was thankful to the hospital staff that someone had thought to give us one of those keepsake boxes.

Also in the keepsake box was a small box with a heart necklace made of stone. The heart was about 1½ inches in size and had a smaller heart cut out from the middle of it. I understood that the larger heart was for me to wear, and the smaller heart was for Zaeden. We tied the smaller heart to his left wrist and I put on the larger heart necklace. What a wonderful gift and how very appropriate.

One of the other things that Children's Hospital said they would do for us was a hand casting of Zaeden. We requested that they do the hand casting of his left hand. That would be an incredible, tangible keepsake to memorialize the handholding and tracings of our love. The staff agreed to our request, and we also asked that the small heart on his left wrist be included in the casting.

Jim had started packing up the things we needed to take from the hospital and had started bringing them to our van. Pastor helped him, and between the two of them they got all of our family's belongings from the waiting area and Zaeden's room. They took all of the handprint pages from the window sill, and the artwork that the kids had taped to the walls, and the books and toys that they had brought for Zaeden.

As the room emptied out, I found myself meticulously searching for things that had been left. I also thought to request a tape measure that we could use to measure Zaeden's height. Carefully and lovingly, we moved Zaeden to measure him. Taralyn's eyes welled with tears as she pointed to an area on Zaeden where blood had already pooled. Closing my eyes to shut out this horrid sight, I fought to keep my breathing rate at a normal level. We both noticed while slightly moving Zaeden, that his body already seemed to be stiffening. The awful realization of his physical death hit harshly and cruelly. Zaeden's physiological death had happened so quickly. Not even an hour before, I had been cradling him softly on my lap, and he was warm and pink. The severity of death and the now coolness and graying color of his body was staggering for me to even attempt to comprehend. Taralyn brought back my attention in asking where the pen was to write the measurement down in his keepsake box. She put the measuring tape, the pen, and the baby lotion we'd used on him into the keepsake box.

I didn't know what else we could have possibly left in the room, and Jim had already left with what he thought was the last of the items to bring to the van. However, I kept going back to

Zaeden and looking through the blankets, and searching on the floor and on the windowsill and everywhere around the room. I felt like we were forgetting something.

When Jim got back in the room, he asked Taralyn and me if we were ready to go. Then it hit me like a punch in the stomach. What I was leaving behind was my baby. My baby Zaeden. My youngest child. I began to cry. Leaving Zaeden's body behind in his hospital room was the hardest thing I ever had to do in my entire life.

# Comfort

My legs wobbled as we walked out of the hospital. I hadn't left the hospital since we'd arrived with Zaeden by ambulance several days before, and the rush of cool, outdoor springtime air seemed surreal. I didn't want to be outdoors. I didn't want to see any people. Frantically, I glanced about, searching for our large, white, twelve-passenger van. Jim gently touched my shoulder and pointed toward a row of vehicles parked in the connected underground parking area. Glancing up at him, I saw that words were not coming easily for him, either. Instinctively my left hand reached out to grab hold of his right hand. Steadying ourselves into a mutually even walking pace, we somberly stepped toward the van. Taralyn had already gotten into the van, and as I climbed into the front passenger seat, I glanced backward toward her to see if she was ready to go. My focus fell instead on the bench seat directly behind me. Zaeden's car seat was gone. Another punch in the stomach. Macrae was the only child we had now that needed a car seat. My stomach lurched.

I faced forward and put on my seat belt with shaky hands. The kids were at the Rainbow House and only Taralyn, Jim, and I were in the van. Along the few blocks to the Rainbow House, I tried to recall the uplifting, strong presence of God and the awesome feeling of Zaeden's spirit going with Jesus. I could clearly remember the event, but my heart was too heavy to feel any of the peace or comfort. I had left Zaeden at the hospital.

Jim parked at the Rainbow House, and I slowly stepped out of the van. I missed having Zaeden with us already, and it was hard to leave the van knowing I would never again unbuckle him from his car seat and carry him with me. I looked up at the late afternoon sky and wished that I, too, could have seen the silver balloon.

I silently begged Zaeden to let me feel his presence. I could no longer put one foot in front of the other and I stopped in the middle of the parking lot, tears streaming down my face. The colors of the day blurred around me, and as I stood there I began to hear the outdoor noises – a car driving by, birds singing. As I looked into the sky the sound of the birds grew louder, as if the air were full of them. However, not a single bird was flying in the sky. They must all be sitting in the tall trees and bushes that surrounded the Rainbow House, I thought. I told myself that they probably seemed louder because I had been indoors for those several past days.

I called to Taralyn and Jim to have them listen to the incredible noise that the birds were making. It seemed like Zaeden was giving me a gift of realizing that birds were all around me even though I couldn't see them. I understood suddenly that Zaeden's spirit was like that, too. Just because I couldn't see him didn't mean that he wasn't with me.

Jim and Taralyn stopped to listen to the birds, and as we began walking toward the Rainbow House again, I thought about the silver balloon. I wanted to see Zaeden's silver balloon. I looked up into the sky, in every direction, but saw nothing except a clear, blue sky that was beginning to show the shadows of a sun moving toward sunset.

With a heavy sigh, I kept walking toward the front entrance of the Rainbow House, and suddenly saw something bright. I blinked a couple of times to try and clear the tears from my eyes. It was something shiny caught in a tree. I looked with fascination at the object in the tree. It was round, but the gentle breeze was wiggling it. A light reflecting off it was a strange, incredible iridescent, silver color. As the object moved, the iridescence seemed to almost magically shimmer. With my eyes finally adjusting to the strange silver light, I suddenly recognized the object. Wow. Oh God! Wow! Another miracle! The object was a silver balloon!

That silver balloon wiggled and squiggled, and waved at me, seeming so happy to have caught my attention. I stared at it, in awe, and noticed that it was completely tangled in the tree. At once, I felt Zaeden telling me, "Mommy, it's all right, I'm right here with you."

Zaeden's strong presence completely overwhelmed me and I stared at the magical shimmering to fully connect with his communication. A peace and comfort settled in, and with excitement I called out to Taralyn and Jim and pointed to the balloon. They both looked at it with disbelief and wonder as all three of us stood and stared at the silver balloon I had so longed to see.

Finally, Jim led me indoors, up some stairs, and down a couple of hallways to find the kids.

We found Grace and Blaes playing a game in a toy room off the kitchen. We then went up some more stairs and down another hallway and found our room. The lights were off and every one of the kids was sleeping. They were spread out on several beds, and on the floor and on the couches. Not wanting to wake them after such a traumatic day, Jim and I went back into the hallway. He led me to a side room and told me I should nap for a little while saying that he would watch the kids. I had been so focused on Zaeden that I hadn't paid much attention to Jim these past days, but now I saw how tired and drawn his face looked. I was blessed to have such a caring husband.

I lay down on the couch and tried to relax. I awoke to darkness. Immediately, I remembered Zaeden's death. I panicked, not knowing where he was, or where I was, or where any of my family was. I got up from the couch and felt dizzy, weak, and nauseous. Then I remembered that we had come to the Rainbow House, and that Jim had led me to that small room. I found the hallway and, after several tries at navigating stairs and other hallways, I finally found him sleeping on a couch next to where Grace and Blaes were still playing. I woke him, asking where the other kids were. I know it caught him completely off guard, and I shouldn't have wakened him, because I knew he needed sleep as much as I did, but the panicky feeling had me kneeling on the floor sobbing.

Jim assured me that the kids were fine and that they were still in the room near where I had been sleeping. However, I couldn't get past the anxiety that I was experiencing. I didn't want Jim to see me like that, so I asked Blaes to show me where the kitchen was, thinking we should get something to eat. I wanted a distraction. Any distraction.

I hadn't eaten anything of substance for the past three days. Blaes found us a couple of cookies, and a frozen ice cream sandwich. We sat at the table, and Grace joined us with a few other snack foods. As I ate with them, I calmed a bit, but the anxiety was just beneath the surface, threatening to erupt.

Jim joined us, and I asked him to lead me back to the side room to talk. I explained to him, while rocking on the floor and crying, that I wanted to talk with a counselor before I got worse. I knew he was trying to understand what I was going through, but I could sense his frustration. He left to request a counselor come to visit us, and then he sat with me. We tried to talk, but words were difficult, and I felt myself pulling inward.

After some time, a counselor arrived. He introduced himself, and I sensed a caring nature. He and Jim sat on the couch, with me still sitting on the floor, crying. He said that he knew what had happened with our family, and that he had done the hand casting of Zaeden. He said that it turned out beautifully. I could tell that he would have done the hand casting with love; just by the way he spoke so tenderly. I cried even more.

I was in deep anguish. I lashed out, asking him why in the world he would do the job he did, listening to delirious people like me in such deep grief. He looked back at me, and gently explained that he wasn't anyone special, but that he always asked God to help him when someone was in need. And, that every time he was with someone in his or her time of need, he seemed to understand a bit more of what God and Heaven were like. He said he tried to use those past experiences every time he was called upon to help someone else, and that over the years he had done the best he could, with God's help, to comfort those in need.

I listened. It seemed profound, yet so simple. He then said that perhaps I didn't realize it, but that I was far, far down into the depths of the valley of the shadow of death. I pondered that for a minute. Yes. I sure was in that valley and death was certainly surrounding my being in every way.

I immediately recognized that from the Bible as being from the 23$^{rd}$ Psalm. I told him that I couldn't remember the words to the 23$^{rd}$ Psalm, and he simply smiled and nodded at me, saying that yes, I could.

I closed my eyes, and started: *"Even though I walk through the valley of the shadow of death..."* And then it was clear to me. *"I fear no evil."*

I kept going: *"For You are with me."* And, yes, I could remember the best part.

*"Your rod and Your staff – they comfort me."* I then remembered the ending verses to the Psalm: *"You prepare a table*

*before me in the presence of my enemies. You anoint my head with oil; my cup overflows. Surely goodness and mercy shall follow me all the days of my life, and I shall dwell in the house of the LORD my whole life long."*

Sudden relief washed over me. I did remember those wonderful words of David. That Psalm now had a dark depth, but also a majestic height that I was just now beginning to understand. It was incredible to connect with the age-old power of God's promises. Yes, I was in the depths of the valley of the shadow of death, but God was with me. I had to figure out how to hold onto that.

The counselor said that over the years he felt that it was his calling to be God's help in providing the rod and staff of comfort to anyone who needed it. I then realized that God had answered yet another prayer of mine. I was comforted.

I explained how awful it had been to watch my baby Zaeden dying. I explained to him that I somewhat knew what Mary the mother of Jesus had felt as she watched Him be crucified on the cross. With a sudden impulse I blurted out that I felt that Mary had the much more difficult cross to bear in watching her Son die. I also said that Mary's suffering was life long, unlike Jesus', and that I couldn't even imagine living a lifetime of such suffering. It seemed too much to bear.

The counselor looked thoughtful at that remark, and then said it would be helpful if I could write down some of my thoughts regarding that. I suddenly received awareness that perhaps I could do that someday. I wondered if my pain was similar to what other parents had experienced with a death of their child. I simultaneously realized that probably not many of those parents had experienced the miracles that our family had received.

A sudden thought occurred to me then that maybe some of the parents were still stuck in the hell that I had been stuck in the first couple of days. Perhaps some parents whose children had died hadn't ever stopped being angry with God and were alone, and in agony. Perhaps those parents didn't know, or didn't believe, or had no hope that their child was now in Heaven with Jesus.

I began to feel a need to reach out as a rod and staff of God to those whom I could comfort.

# Insanity

It was past 10:00 p.m. at this point, and I was calm and clear of mind again. Jim and I told the counselor how thankful we were that he had taken the time to visit with us and comfort us. When he left, I was ready to be with the kids. I knew I needed to be strong for them, and now I felt that I had strength again.

As we walked into the room that had been reserved for our family, I saw that all of the kids were still asleep. They lay sprawled everywhere, and even in their sleep they looked completely exhausted and grieved.

Jim and I then settled into a bed that Macrae was lying on because I knew that he would wake in the night and I needed to be near him. It seemed so strange, having that big room so full of our family, yet seeming so empty without Zaeden sleeping amongst us. I cried as softly as I could.

In the middle of the night I awoke to a ferocious wind that blew through the windows that the kids had left open when they went to sleep. I sat up, and in an instant recalled the horrible reason our whole family was sleeping at the Rainbow House. Immediately, tears fell, and an overwhelming grief left me barely able to walk across the room to close the windows. In the darkness of night, I had to step across kids as they lay with pillows and blankets, scattered all around the big room. As I closed each window, the wind seemed to get stronger, and as the last one was closed the rain began to fall. Huge drops splashed against the now closed windows, and an angry, wild wind pounded them. I looked outside, and saw the trees bending and swaying in the relentless wind.

As I looked around the room again, I saw all the kids at once. The room was filled with kids, my family, my loved ones. But, for as full as it was, it was also empty.

Zaeden was not in his pajamas lying in my bed. The deepness of that emptiness is so hard to describe. I've seen an empty cup when my kids ask me to fill it with milk. I know that when the gas gauge is close to empty, I need to stop at a gas station soon. With all of the house moves we've made, I know what a strange feeling it is to walk out of a now empty house for the last time, and then walk into an empty house that we are moving into and feel happy.

With all of those, "empty" is something that has a container: a cup, a gas tank, and a house. But, the emptiness of a person seems entirely different. I had never before experienced my spirit being empty, and it scared me. I also then thought about seeing Zaeden's body in the hospital after his spirit went with Jesus, and thought about how his body was empty of his spirit.

As I got back into bed, feeling the warmth of Macrae's body against me, the story of Jesus and Lazarus came to mind. Knowing that Jesus was close to Lazarus and his sisters, Mary and Martha, it always seemed strange to me that when Jesus heard that Lazarus was dying, He waited several days before going to be with them. It seemed deserved that upon His arrival, the sisters greeted Him with deep grief and resentment, saying that if He had been there, their brother would not have died.

Jesus tries to reassure them with His presence, saying that anyone who believes in Him would never die. Lazarus had been in the tomb four days, and walking toward Him, "Jesus wept".

I paused as I recalled that part of the story. The shortest verse in the Bible: Jesus wept. How powerful now to me, knowing that Jesus was saddened to the point of weeping as He embraced those who loved Lazarus and grieved with them. Jesus understood the physical connection we have with those we love! And He knew, He felt, He understood how empty it feels not to have a loved one with us physically.

I drew closer to Jesus at that moment than I ever had before. Because, of course, Jesus knew that Lazarus was alive in spirit for eternity, but in human form He also knew how special it is being alive physically.

I felt the presence of Jesus so strongly at that moment, as strongly as when I was holding Zaeden in his last moments. The gift of that presence is an overwhelming experience, but the understanding came to me then that the humanness of this world could quickly push it aside. How quickly the physical realm can overtake the spiritual.

Realizing this, I admonished myself. Our family had been blessed, so blessed with God's presence and peace in that hospital. How quickly I'd gone down to the depths of grief again, and then up toward the profoundness of that peace. Down again. Up again. What a hideous, mind-bending, timeless tug of war within myself.

Understanding that this battle was still happening to me was a fresh insight that brought with it a bit of knowledge. Could I try to hold on to the peace and mercy and God's presence even as I kept taking step after step through the valley of the shadow of death?

Having those gyrations of the past several days rocketing through my head as I tried to sleep again made me anxious and so gut-wrenchingly sickened. How horrible the images of a dying loved one, of grieving siblings, of helplessness expressed so deeply. How could I clear my head of those images? It seemed even as I tried to clear them, more would take their places. *Oh God, help me.*

I awakened and noticed that the daylight was new, and fresh, and soft, and color was coming into the room. I remembered the beautiful, mysterious, shimmering colors of the balloon that I'd seen just outside the Rainbow House yesterday. That balloon! I wanted to see it again. And I remembered the harsh storm that had violently blown through during the night. I wanted to have that balloon. I needed to keep that balloon. It was a miracle balloon. It was so beautiful with all those shimmering colors, just like I imagined Heavenly beauty to be. I had to get that balloon!

It was before sunrise, and as I ran out the door of the Rainbow House, I realized that no one else was even awake yet. Frantically, I looked to the side of the Rainbow House toward the area where the balloon had been stuck in the tree just the day before. My heart plummeted – the balloon was nowhere to be seen in the tree. The winds were so strong during the night that it probably had blown out of the tree. I looked on the ground around the trees. No luck. I walked around the side of the Rainbow House. It wasn't there. I walked across the street, but I didn't see the balloon anywhere.

At this point, desperation took over common sense, and I walked up to bushes, and looked under cars, and in between houses, frantically searching for the balloon. No luck. I walked up and down two blocks and then circled back another way to the Rainbow House parking lot. I looked throughout the parking lot and all around the block where the trees were. Perhaps the balloon had blown up into another tree and gotten stuck again.

The cool air and drizzly rain had soaked me and I couldn't stop shivering. I needed that balloon! Where was it? I was cold and numb and my walking had become sluggish as the sun rose. I lost hope. I walked toward the parking lot and looked under the cars one last time. I checked the van to make sure it had been locked the night before, and re-traced my steps taken yesterday toward the Rainbow House. How different this morning: no birds singing, no gentle breeze, no bright sunshine, and no balloon.

As I looked at the sky, it seemed as dismal and dreary as my spirit. Tears spilled uncontrollably and I slowly made my way back to the Rainbow House. As I took the last steps, I glanced upward toward the tree where the balloon had been yesterday. Through my tears, I saw a grey object in a tree closer to the building. Blinking to clear the tears, I looked again at what the object could be. I ran closer to get a better look. Incredible. It appeared to be a balloon, or rather what was left of a balloon. As I stood directly in front of the tree, and looking straight upward at the object, it was obvious that the object was indeed a balloon.

What a sad, pitiful sight it was now, though. The balloon hung limply about 30 feet above me, with its curly ribbons tangled in a small branch. I stared upward in disbelief. This couldn't be the same balloon that just yesterday had radiated Heavenly spiritual light, could it? What had happened? I tried to see the detail of the balloon, but realized that it was simply too high to distinguish.

I wanted to see that balloon more closely. I inspected the pattern of growth on the tree. Drat! The tree had a huge trunk and the lower limbs must have been decades old. All of the limbs were too high for me to climb. If I took a run at it and jumped, could I reach one of the limbs? Then common sense took over. It would be impossible. And with the bark being wet, trying to climb that tree would be not only foolish, but dangerous as well. I sighed, but the strong need to have that balloon persisted. What to do?

As I walked through the doors of the Rainbow House toward the front desk, I saw the receptionist staring at me with curious concern. It occurred to me then that my wet clothes and hair and tear-stained face must be quite a sight. Not in the least deterred, however, I boldly asked if she could do me a favor. An idea had occurred to me. As I explained it to her, I saw the same "what-in-the-world?" expression that Jim had whenever I approached him with one of my "ideas."

The young woman politely stated that she was just the receptionist and that she didn't know what could be done. A helpless anxiety washed through me and I realized that she saw that on my face. She added, sympathetically, that the manager had just arrived and perhaps I could speak with her about my request.

The same expression of curious concern appeared on the manager's face as I entered her office. This time, though, I had trouble even voicing my idea. The emotion and need and exhaustion and being soaking cold took over, and I felt far away as I tried to explain what I'd hoped for.

I could see that she knew about our family's situation with Zaeden, and that she wanted to help. But, it was also clear that she was at a loss as to what to do. She said she would try to help, and as I watched her perplexed expression, I understood the craziness of my request. Embarrassed, I apologized and said that I appreciated her time and having listened to my request, but I understood that it was probably not to be.

I numbly made my way toward the staircase, and wondered how in the world I'd find our room again. Then I saw Jim walking toward me, looking worried and exhausted and grieved. He put his long arms around me and hugged me, both of us relieved to see the other. As we held each other, he explained that the kids were awake, and most of them had eaten breakfast. They were now in the process of packing up and getting ready for us to go home. He urged me to get something to eat, but I didn't have an appetite.

He knew I'd been outside because of how wet and cold I was, and with concern he asked what I'd been doing. I explained the saga of looking for the balloon, and then finding it. As I reported the trail of determination, anxiety, hopelessness, joy, relief, excitement, and then embarrassment, I saw that he was simply too exhausted to follow the story. I ended it by saying that I realized it was a dumb idea, and I wanted to see the kids and change into some dry clothes. He picked up the bag full of our belongings that he'd earlier intended to bring out to the van, and pointed me in the direction of our room.

In our room, a couple of the kids were wrestling with pillows, a couple of them were telling them to sit down and be quiet, and others were trying to gather belongings that had been scattered everywhere. Chaos is a good word for our family, and at that moment I clearly saw it. I saw and felt what most other people probably see and feel when walking into our home. It was overwhelming. This was an odd feeling for me, but now it seemed difficult to focus on all that commotion happening simultaneously.

As I stood there, I sighed, realizing that we'd been away from our home, confined to hospital quiet and orderliness for four days. Of course the kids needed some letting loose of that. We all needed that. Macrae ran over to me and hugged me tightly. I hugged him as tight as I could and it was wonderful to be able to share that. The other kids settled down as soon as they saw me, and we exchanged sad smiles as each of us quietly decided on separate areas of the room to pack up our belongings and tidy up.

Nobody had words to say, and yet we didn't want the silence, either. An uncomfortable commotion replaced the quiet as some of the kids called to the others to help find something of theirs, or an older child admonished a younger one to not be lazy and to help pack up. The strain was visible in faces, voices, and motions.

I struggled, trying to be the mom that I knew I should be, and wanted to be, for them. I searched in vain to find and speak the words that could help us get through this. It seemed, though, that exhaustion had finally taken hold of me and I couldn't shake any sensible words loose. My throat was tight and my stomach seized up in knots.

I realized then, that there was not one word, or touch, or hug, or anything that would make this better. Letting go of that expectation gave me the clarity of mind to simply voice encouragement for the kids to work together and be kind to each other.

Perhaps the tiredness in my voice was what they needed. Everyone became more focused and they quickly emptied the room of our belongings and carried the loads out to the van.

One of the kids ran in the room shouting to me that dad said I should come outside right away. I don't even recall which child it was, as I fought panic and fear that something bad had happened outside. Maybe one of the kids had gone out into the street. Or maybe a car in the parking lot hadn't seen one of the little ones walking toward the van! I dropped what I was doing and sprinted down the stairs, finding Jim just outside the entry of the Rainbow House.

As I ran toward him, he turned to me, smiling the biggest smile I'd seen in a long while. Saying nothing, he just pointed toward the side of the building. The panic subsided as soon as I saw his smile, but it was quickly replaced with embarrassment as I saw a huge utility truck with a long lift parked at the edge of the parking lot. The driver got out, expressing mild disbelief as he gazed upward toward the tree. Jim looked at me with the same look of disbelief, but also with an underlying happy relief.

As the logic of what was happening sunk in, the embarrassment level rose even higher. It was obvious that the manager had gone to an extreme to help grant the request I'd tearfully asked for less than an hour ago. I'd wanted her to help me find a way to get the balloon unstuck from that tree. I'd explained the story of the silver balloon above the hospital and seeing such a beautiful balloon outside of the Rainbow House yesterday.

I'd only expected her to perhaps call the janitorial staff and get a ladder that I could climb on to get up into the tree. She'd gotten a ladder all right. But it was a very long ladder, and was attached to a utility truck. A utility truck such as this is normally seen working high up on electric lines or on telephone poles. A utility truck such as this is not normally seen rescuing balloons out of trees for a grieving parent.

As soon as the driver saw me, he knew it was me that was the reason he'd been paged out so early on a Saturday morning to rescue a bedraggled silver balloon! His eyes glanced over at me with skeptical, incredulous disbelief, but then displayed a quiet, professional demeanor. I could do no more than stand silently by that truck, shivering and embarrassed and desperately needful of that balloon.

The driver pulled levers, heaved this and that, pulled levers again, got in and out of the cab, and a gait of frustration was soon noticeable in the back and forth motions. Jim asked if there was anything he could do to help. The driver relayed the bad news expressed with hopelessness. The truck lift was stuck.

Jim cast a look toward me that pleaded a "please-tell-the-driver-thank-you-for-trying-and-that-he-can-go-home-now" look. I sighed, and realized the true stupidity of what I'd requested of the staff, and the time and effort it had cost them and the driver. Hot shame washed over me and the grieving heaved up from the depths of me with a deep anguish. Tears streamed down my face. As I tried to clear them away to go speak with the driver, I heard a strange mechanical noise. Blinking the blurred vision away, I tried to see where the driver was, but before I could spot him, a movement caught my attention. The lift was moving upward.

The driver was beaming and gracefully raised that monstrous tool upward toward the limb that held the silver balloon captive. Daring not to breathe, not to move, not to speak, I willed the lift to please, please, please keep lifting. *Please, please, dear God please, keep the lift working its way toward the balloon!*

The noise quieted and the driver was soon reaching hands outward to rescue the balloon. As we squinted upward it was clearly noticeable that the ribbon strings were tangled this way and that, with curls and knots aplenty. The driver, having the advantage of surveying the situation up close, quickly went with plan B. Pulling a clipper from his tool belt; he simply clipped off the small branch that tethered the balloon in place.

With branch tightly in hand, and balloon still tangled securely to it, he maneuvered his way down from the precarious height. As he presented the branch and balloon to Jim, his expression quietly relayed an overall sense of relief mixed with the satisfaction of having helped someone in need.

With a nod of thanks to the driver, and not another word, Jim handed me the branch and balloon. Then, visibly still shaken by this event, he walked toward the kids, helping them load the last of our belongings in the van.

Silent relief waved through me, and from that depth, the grief quieted, and gratitude swelled outward. The next moment I was at the driver's side thanking him and hugging him and thanking him again. A look of understanding passed between us that what had been rescued was not just a bedraggled balloon, but a treasure of immeasurable value.

As the driver pulled his rig out of the parking lot, I looked down at the tangle of branch and string and balloon. Immediate shock rocked through my senses. This balloon had not only been battered by the storm, it had obviously been tangled in that tree for quite some time! The colors were completely muted and even washed to a dull film in places. How could that be? The balloon I'd seen yesterday radiated iridescence and sparkling silvery light. How could this be the same balloon?

Jim called gently to me that all our belongings were packed and that it was time to go home. I asked him to please wait for a minute, as I turned toward the door of the Rainbow House. The manager greeted me with a joy that is only felt when a genuine gift of caring has been given to someone. "Thank you" didn't seem to be enough, yet I suddenly understood that it also wasn't needed.

Stammering, I tried to relay how much their time and efforts meant to me, and I asked what the cost of the driver and truck would be so that we could pay them. The manager waved me toward the door, and simply smiled, saying that the lady for whom the Rainbow House had been built would want this to be her gift to our family. Tears flowed freely again, and I completely understood the purity of giving from the heart.

In silence, I climbed into the van, the tangles of branch and balloon clutched tightly to my chest. I pondered the events of yesterday's sighting of that glorious silver balloon. As I slowly remembered the details of walking toward the Rainbow House and my sight being drawn to the iridescent sparkling, I realized that it had been yet another blessing.

Something that beautiful could not be of this world. Something that beautiful was a glimpse of what had been beyond the balloon, and had radiated toward me through that balloon. The overwhelming understanding joined with the now-familiar and powerful presence that we'd felt holding Zaeden in those last moments. I understood. We'd been gifted with a glimpse of Heaven – the profound magnificence of Zaeden's spiritual presence with Jesus radiating through a balloon that someone had let loose long ago, tangled into a tree beside the Rainbow House until our family needed it.

# Answered Prayers

During the drive home from the Rainbow House that Saturday morning with the once radiant, now bedraggled, balloon sitting limply on my lap, I glanced over at Jim. Over the years our family has traveled many thousands of miles, experiencing the close togetherness that naturally occurs when packing a large family into a not-large-enough van. Jim has always assumed the role of driver, and has seemed content to be in charge of the mechanics of getting us from point A to point B. I accepted the responsibility long ago of having to initiate conversation with him during our drive times. Usually, I would ramble on and on about some topic of interest to me, and he would listen attentively without feeling compelled to respond.

This drive, though, had me at a loss. Glancing in his direction, I noticed Jim's resolute expression, leading me to understand that this drive home was a special mission for him – something he wanted to do for his family. I felt a deep appreciation mixed with envy. He was able to do something for our family. I had no idea what to do.

I had no idea how to even start a conversation. What topic was important enough that it deserved the effort of conversation? In numb silence, my thoughts stalled.

Jim caught my glance, and we exchanged a quiet togetherness of our souls with harmonious understanding that no words were necessary. His attention returned to the road ahead, but I didn't want to look at the road ahead, much less travel it. I turned to look at him again, not quite knowing why, but just wanting to. As my gaze rested on his profile, I became aware that his face registered differently – haggard, grieved, bereft. I was shocked to realize how much our emotions affect us physically. Jim bore the mark of someone who had experienced the death of one whom he had cherished beyond his own life. It had aged him.

A deep and defeated realization struck me that the mark of "aging" had probably also been permanently stamped upon me. I have never liked my physical appearance. In fact, I have been embarrassed by it, in spite of assurances by others that I am not unattractive. My sisters were gifted with beauty, but not me. I am continually grateful that none of our children have been cursed with my unattractive features. I shudder to think how I will look when the natural aging process accentuates my features even more.

With that thought, I pulled down the visor and snapped open the compact mirror. I could only stare at the image before me. "Aged" didn't do justice to what I saw. I was shocked at the deep emptiness reflected in my eyes, coupled with a complete absence of expression.

The television portrayal of a starving child in a third world country came to mind; then, the face of an anguished adult in a country being torn apart by war. Their expressions seemed to have depth far beneath the facial features.

It is said that the eyes are the window to our soul. I have often looked into a person's eyes to gauge the clarity or truth of what their words and body language were saying. As a mom, it is a great tool that I've used many times. I saw now that the experience our family had gone through within the past four days had left us devoid of expression. And in that absence, our souls were now openly exposed.

I turned in my seat and looked at each of my children's faces. The term "raw emotion" came to mind. Each person in our family bore this mark – the same expression as seen on those TV photos. Capturing those expressions clearly speaks to the state of a person, and it is no wonder that journalists search for that in their photography.

I looked at myself in the mirror again, and saw my "self" – my soul. Strangely, my physical appearance didn't even jump out at me this time. I didn't react with the usual embarrassment that I felt when seeing myself in the mirror while brushing my teeth, or in a family photograph, or when brushing my hair and putting on makeup. No, embarrassment was not my reaction. My heart tugged painfully as my eyes revealed my soul's expression. I studied them intently and realized that this was the real me. My inner self. My soul. I felt a connection, a strange but wonderful oneness, with that expression of soul. Allowing myself to connect with that depth gave me a new freedom to be completely dismissive of my physical characteristics. None of that seemed to matter anymore.

Relief washed over me. I had just now been able to separate my "physical" from my "spiritual" self. Wow! I realized that my physical being is of lesser value than my spiritual being.

Looking at Jim, and then at the kids, it was as if I had been awakened to a higher level of understanding. I remembered seeing Zaeden lying on my lap even after his physical death, knowing his spirit was no longer confined to his body. I could see the difference now. It was as if my eyes were being given the gift of sight for the first time. My children – how beautiful their expressions – their souls. Now open for me to clearly see. And I looked and looked at them. And I looked at Jim as he drove the many miles home, and I clearly saw him – his beautiful soul.

I no longer simply saw the strong connection of our family. I experienced it. I felt it. I heard it in each of their voices. I heard the love, and the aching, and the reaching out, and the helplessness, and the anguish.

As our van ate up the miles, my thoughts went back in time. Placing so much emphasis on my physical self seemed such a sad waste of so many years. And for what? I didn't know the answer.

Jim pulled off the Interstate and I began to panic. Only ten more minutes and we would be home where so many memories of Zaeden were everywhere. Zaeden had been born in my bedroom of that house. The kids had seen him for the first time in our living room, only a few minutes old. Zaeden was our littlest buddy, our little Zaedy Bear that always came running up to us the minute we first came in the door. How could we go into that house and not hear his voice, see him running full speed at us, and hugging us tightly? How could we do that?

Grief rolled thunderously, pounding my emotions. Tears accompanied the panic, and spasms of pain rolled through me. I wanted to scream! I needed to. This awful, hideous emotion could not stay inside of me. It felt as if it was destroying me, eating at my insides, ripping my guts to shreds.

The panic rose higher. I sobbed, and heaved with those sobs, the awfulness of knowing that Zaeden would not be at home to ever greet us like that ever again. Never again. I could not survive "never again." *God. Oh dear God.* My mind screamed to Him that I could not survive this. I couldn't!

Jim reached over and put his hand in mine. He squeezed tight, and I noticed tears flowing down his cheeks, too. Neither of us could stop that flow, and we could not let loose of each other's hands. We clung to each other through the tight grip.

I turned to the kids and saw the look of pain on Macrae's face as he fought to hold back tears. Damn it! Damn it all! My sobbing had rippled back toward the kids. *Dear God. I don't know how to get through this. How am I supposed to help my children through this?* What could I do or say to Jim and the kids to help them? *Lord, God, help me once again. Show me what to do or say to make this easier. This is going to be so hard.*

Jim squeezed my hand again, this time with noticeable firmness, and with that, both of us knew we needed to pull ourselves together. Somehow. Or at least push all of the pain inside for a while for the sake of the kids. How we would get through this remained unanswered. I was too weary and battered to even think of a plan.

I reached around toward Macrae to take hold of his hand. He was holding onto a dinosaur. He shifted it to his other hand and I noticed some other toys scattered on the seat and also on the floor. Some of those toys were newer, and some were bought many years ago, probably for one of the older kid's birthdays. That had never seemed to matter. The kids simply passed the "little kid toys" down to whoever was that age. So it was that Macrae and Zaeden had many, many "little kid toys."

Still holding Macrae's hand, my mind wandered to the many things in our house that belonged to Macrae and Zaeden. The house would have so many of those reminders. I quickly realized that it would be painful seeing all of that everywhere in the house.

An idea popped into mind. I held up Macrae's dinosaur and showed the kids. Then I smiled, as best I could, and tried to voice an excitement that I truly wanted to express but didn't really feel. I had the kids' attention. Their eyes were focused on me, and I realized I had better come up with something good, some really good plan, something they would be able to feel good about. *God, please help me. I need You to help us get through going into our house. Right now, God! I need you!*

Even before I was done praying, the idea fully came to me. I began talking with the kids about how we had so many things in our house that Zaeden loved. I said that we might be getting visitors and it would be really good if we could find as many of Zaeden's things that we could, so we could keep them together. Then, I said we could get a special cabinet with lights in it and we could always keep Zaeden's toys and stuff safe for him. The younger kids' eyes became bright with excitement, as I explained that we could do this "treasure hunt" for Zaeden right away when we got home.

They began to talk amongst themselves about this or that toy they knew was in this or that place in the house. It seemed they each had special things they would look for or knew where to look. I also asked them if they could each find a toy or something that was really special between just them and Zaeden that they might want to give to him and that he could keep with him. The kids' thoughts gave smiles to their expressions. I asked Grace if she had a toy in mind that she wanted to look for. She was about to answer when Macrae interrupted, and soon all of the kids were talking excitedly about the many things they were remembering and what they each wanted to choose.

As we pulled into Elk Horn and then into our driveway, I interrupted their talking and asked them where we should put all of Zaeden's special things when we found them. We decided the best place would be in the dining room on the ping-pong table.

I also let them know that when they'd found all those things throughout the house, and chosen something special for Zaeden to keep with him, that they should come find me and show it to me.

At those words, Jim was parking the van in our driveway behind the house. The kids started tumbling out of the van. Soon after, the arguing began for this one to hurry up, and that one not to step on this one's foot. Inevitably, someone was holding up the entire process by looking for a shoe that had been taken off and was now lost and that person was "in the way" of everyone else who needed to get out of the van.

I released a long sigh, along with an intense prayer of thanks. I knew where the idea for a treasure hunt had come from, and I was extremely thankful to God. The kids ran up the sidewalk, enthusiastically calling out and racing each other to begin the treasure hunt.

# Embarrassment

I grabbed a few handfuls of things that had been scattered on the floor in the front area of the van, as well as the balloon and branch, and headed quickly up the walk to the house. I was barely one step into the doorway when a couple of the kids met me, eagerly announcing toys they'd already found. Congratulating them, I reminded them to put the toys on the ping-pong table. They turned from me and raced off to find more treasures.

After the next few steps into the doorway, I was taken aback by the sight of the dining room. I glanced around the room, and feared what had happened in our house while we'd been gone. Walking a few steps further, I heard voices in the kitchen and noticed an aroma of cleaning products.

I entered the kitchen. Glancing this way and that, I realized my fear had actually occurred. Both the dining room and kitchen were sparkling clean!

I tried to smile at the women who were standing in the kitchen, but my nervous fears gave way to complete embarrassment. I knew very well that our house seldom, if ever, looked like the dining room and kitchen now looked. Usually, we had stuff lying or stacked all over. Our busy schedules never seemed to allow the time or energy to organize and deal with the never-ending messes.

I walked back into the dining room and nearly collided with a couple of the kids as they ran in with newly found Zaeden treasures to show me. As they ran back out of the dining room to find more things, I stood silently and closed my eyes.

*God, I do not want all of this to be happening.* My throat felt tight. Still holding the balloon in hand, I focused my thoughts on it. I carefully and tenderly placed the bedraggled balloon and branch on top of our upright piano, where I knew it should be safe from being played with or accidentally thrown into the trash by someone who didn't know its priceless value.

I had to let go of my grief, but that was really difficult. I knew I had to focus on the swirling chaos in our house, but I really didn't want to. Already, though, more of the kids were running to show me what they'd now found of Zaeden's. Stories that he'd played with this toy or that with them tumbled out of their memories, and they smiled in sharing them with each other and me. Those were happy memories. I forced my mind to think about those happy times and rise above the grief that wanted to surface, knowing that those times would never happen again.

Macrae walked into the dining room holding two large toy monsters, one that was his and one that was Zaeden's. I could see by his confused expression that he didn't quite know if he needed to put both of them on the ping-pong table. He knew that those monsters belonged together; that he and Zaeden had always played with both of those monsters together.

My little Macrae. His thoughtfulness relaxed me. Smiling at him with genuine understanding, I asked him what he wanted to do. He decided to keep both of them in the toy box, because that way the toys could still play together. I agreed, patting him on his behind, and he ran back to the toy box with both monsters held tight.

Bracing myself, I went into the kitchen again. Women were busy arranging food on the table and drying dishes. Our large kitchen table, where we usually ate our family meals, was completely covered with assorted containers of food. A few of the women were helping the kids fill their plates. I saw lunchmeat, breads, condiments, salads, chips, desserts, and plastic tableware. I couldn't even fathom how much food was stacked all over the table and counters of the kitchen, much less where all that food had come from.

One of the women in the kitchen, a good friend of mine, caught my embarrassed glance. Walking over to me, she quietly said that several of the ladies had come into our house over the past days and had done some cleaning. I could have fallen onto the floor, realizing how much effort that must have taken to clean our house.

As we looked into each other's eyes, though, I knew. And, I knew that she knew. It was a gift from them to us. It was what they had wanted to do for our family. It was what they knew they could do for our family, when they hadn't known what else to do. Tears welled up in my eyes, but I quickly brushed them away when I saw that she looked about to cry, as well.

This was no time to cry. This was a time to acknowledge the gift and the givers for their selfless acts of kindness. She and I both knew what effort they had put into cleaning our house, but I could see from looking into her eyes, that it didn't matter one bit. I was not to be embarrassed. I understood they had wanted to help us. And that's what the focus needed to be on, because they had been a tremendous help.

We hugged with heartfelt thankfulness replacing my embarrassment. I realized I wouldn't have had the strength of mind or physical stamina to clean our house in the coming days. I hadn't even thought of it needing to be done prior to when I'd walked into the house.

Already, someone was knocking on the front door, and someone else went quickly out of the kitchen to answer it. Soon another guest had come, carrying yet another armful of food. Another stab of embarrassment pained me. I followed the ladies into the kitchen, and seeing this gift being placed with all of the other food overwhelmed me. I voiced squeaky thankfulness to the ladies who stood in the kitchen. It was met with a chorus of "It wasn't much," and "We were happy to help," and "Anytime," and "We can come over for as much as you need us to help with the food or cleaning."

The ladies in the kitchen busied themselves again being attentive to feeding the kids. Seeing that the ladies had everything completely under control, and also that they were, in fact, dismissing me from helping the kids get their plates filled, I walked out of the kitchen.

It was then, walking into the hallway and living room, that I noticed the laundry baskets of folded, clean laundry. Oh no! They couldn't have... No! They wouldn't have! Whirling around, with my mind fixed on dispelling what I already knew had to have happened, I re-traced my steps into the kitchen. Glancing neither right nor left, I made a mad dash toward the door to the basement, and hoped that that no one noticed my panicked expression.

Racing down the stairs, I landed on the cement floor with a jolt. I turned to the right, pleading to see the familiar deplorable condition of mountains of dirty clothes. My fears were realized, yet again.

The huge piles of dirty laundry and table full of unsorted clean clothes and dirty sink and shower were no more. They had been picked up, cleaned up, washed, folded, scrubbed, and who knows what else. I didn't even want to think that others had seen this ugly basement with its many loads of dirty laundry.

This was a consequence of our large family living in a house that was not large enough. We hadn't ever been able to afford a double set of washers and dryers and the basement wasn't fit with plumbing or electricity for that, anyway.

When we bought the house we hadn't cared about the basement condition, because we were going to build a new basement when the house was moved to the farm. That was the plan and was more my dream than Jim's. And I knew that the consequences of this basement were more my fault than his. The deplorable conditions were my guilt, too. I worked full time and was also the best full time mom that I could be. That didn't include always getting all the laundry done. Still, we hadn't been able to save up enough money to move the house and build a basement that would organize our laundry and eliminate the water issues.

Oh dear God! This was an absolute and complete embarrassment! Jim and I had not ever, ever let anyone go into our basement except the plumber who was routinely called upon when we couldn't get the drain unclogged or the shower to stop leaking again.

I realized the women who had come into the basement only wanted to help us get the laundry washed. I knew they would be kind-hearted enough to overlook the deplorable conditions. But yet, it was my mess. My secret mess. My deplorable space in my house and my secret. I didn't want anyone to know about it! I didn't want to be so embarrassed and ashamed of how awful I am at keeping our house clean and organized.

I sank to the floor. My head was pounding with horrible thoughts that even the quiet of the basement couldn't still. Sitting in the aloneness of that empty basement seemed somehow appropriate. I wanted to be alone. I just wanted everyone to leave me alone. I didn't want anyone to see me or talk to me or be near me.

After a few minutes the cold, damp floor created a sharp, uncomfortable pain in the hot, tight muscle in my leg. Pulling my knees close, and resting my head on them, I closed my eyes again. I didn't want to see any more. I didn't want this to be happening. I didn't want to have women upstairs taking care of my kids and helping get them fed. I didn't want any of this to have happened.

Tears fell silently. I didn't know if anyone had noticed me walking down the stairs to the basement, but I was hoping that they hadn't. I just needed to sit for a little while, by myself. Somehow, in the ugliness and cold and dreariness of that awful basement, I felt a kinship. My thoughts were ugly and cold and dreary and awful, too.

I had spent so many hours in this ugly dirty basement. Several years before, I'd placed enough shelving in the basement for each member of our family's clothes. How many loads of laundry had I sorted, washed, dried, folded, and stacked onto those shelves? I did try to do well with the laundry, but over the years, it had just become madness, and it was all I could do to maintain my balance, much less my sanity, as I stumbled over continuous mountains of laundry in the never-ending battle with the clothes.

That was one of my most well kept secrets, though. Because the clothes were contained in the basement, we didn't have too much of a clothes mess upstairs. And everyone in the family knew the big rule – never, ever, under any circumstance, let anyone except the plumber or close friends of the kids' venture into that ugliness of the basement.

Life had been so busy, and I was so tired most days, that I had been content to let it be the ugliness that it was. I knew I should have tried harder to deal with the clothing challenges. But, I hadn't. I'd felt guilty all these years about our horrible secret with the basement. Now, I imagined all of the women in the entire community had walked into our basement and seen the awful ugliness and horrific laundry condition. Now they knew our secret.

Still sitting on that now cleanly-swept, but still cold and always damp floor, I felt my embarrassment turn to shame, and the tears stung as they fell, because I knew that if I'd tried harder in the past, been a better mother, washed three loads a day minimum, that now the basement would be in decent shape. I hadn't, though and it wasn't. I hadn't wanted to be in that dingy basement washing three loads of clothes each day, though.

Time was so precious, and instead I'd always found myself wanting to be in the kitchen cooking up a big meal or cookies for a family treat. Or I would snuggle with the kids at bedtime, when magically their needs would be remembered. I would then need to sign a field-trip form, or need to help with a math equation, or take out a just-noticed sliver, or whatever else the kids would come up with. The strange thing was though, that during the rush of dealing with all those superficial bed-time voiced needs, words and events also tumbled out that I came to know were actually the true needs of each child. One of the kids' friends spilled an entrusted secret, or another of them had gotten a bad quiz grade, or one of them would share the pain of not being invited to a birthday party. No, I hadn't wanted to be in a dingy basement stuck in an awful, musty laundry room when my kids needed me upstairs. I had made that choice consciously. Now this was the humiliating consequence.

Staring at the empty floor, I became aware of what also was no longer there. *My* dirty clothes. Someone had taken those, as well. The pounding of my heart doubled and then tripled to a panic level. The thought of someone else washing my clothes and under things was over the edge for me to think about! Jim and the kids knew better than to ever wash and dry my clothes. I always did my own laundry and always knew where my clothes were. No, this couldn't have happened. But, I saw that indeed it had happened. The shelf for my clean clothing was nearly empty and the mound of my dirty clothes was nowhere to be seen.

My place of solitude and refuge where I could cry alone was no more. I had to get out of the basement immediately. Racing thoughts came to mind. Did I dare to even bathe, not knowing if I had any clean underwear or clothes to change into anywhere in the house? And if they weren't in our house, whose house were they at?

Racing up the stairs two and three at a time, I halted suddenly when reaching the doorway to the kitchen. Again, I felt the need not to be seen by anyone in the kitchen, but this time for a different reason. Shame forced me to look down. I should never have let the laundry or our house get this messy and disorganized.

It didn't matter that for the past several months the school and church calendar had our family running all directions almost every night of the week. It didn't matter that I worked full time. I should have somehow managed my household better, but I hadn't. That was a total embarrassment, and humiliating to admit.

With my eyes fixed on forward and hasty steps directed toward my bedroom, I succeeded in getting from the basement to the second story of our house without being called out to. I walked into the bedroom, closed the door, and sank heavily onto the bed. Closing my eyes, I let myself just lie there. A weight seemed to have pressed me into that bed, preventing movement. Truly though, I had no desire to move even one tiny muscle. I needed to, just absolutely needed to, simply lie there.

It was Saturday afternoon. In the previous nights and days since Tuesday evening, I hadn't had many hours of sleep. It seemed a blur now. Not even desiring to clear the focus of those days and nights, I just lay motionless on my bed.

A strong sense of remembrance flooded my memory. Sighing a deep and soft and sad exhale, I recalled that just 2 ½ years ago, I had given birth to Zaeden right here in this bedroom on this bed. *Oh dear Heavenly God.*

I remembered the intense pain of impending childbirth and anxiety of knowing we'd never get to the hospital in time. I barely made it to the bed in time. Earlier, contractions had become regular and we'd called our friend Lisa to come to our house and stay with

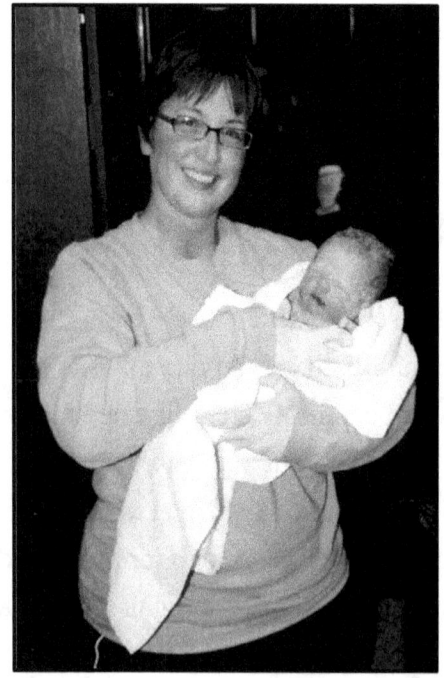

the kids so that we could leave for the hospital. Now, Lisa was urging me to stay calm. We both knew how to birth babies. She is an OB nurse and she knew what to do, but having him birthed in our bed was not planned. A minute later Zaeden was born into her loving hands. I remember Lisa saying that he was beautiful and perfect and a miracle. Yes, indeed.

Jim had called 911, but didn't make it back to the bedroom in time to see Zaeden born. Jim cut his cord and Lisa swaddled him tight and warmly with baby blankets they found in the suitcase I'd packed for the hospital. She and Jim brought Zaeden downstairs to meet his brothers and sisters. They all saw Zaeden before I did! Jim told me later how scared, yet excited, they were to see their newly born baby brother. The rescue squad arrived in the midst of 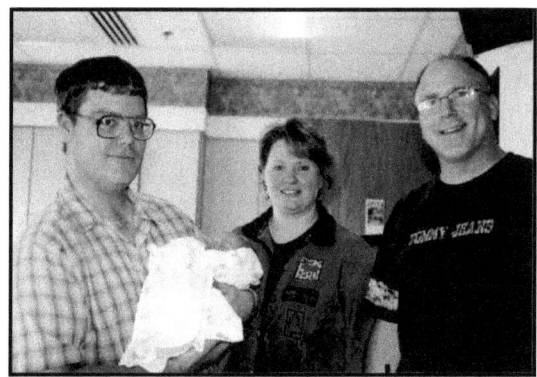 all that excitement. I was so thankful to see so many of my fellow EMTs! They helped calm everyone, treated Zaeden and me, and ensured that our vitals were stable. With joy and wonderful, professional care, Zaeden and I were soon loaded into the ambulance and safely being transported to the local hospital.

I remembered lying on the bed, feeling emptied of the child I'd just born. I felt that same profound sense of emptiness now, as I lay motionless on that same bed. This time I was alone in the room, though, and the emptiness seemed larger. Much larger and deeper and heavier. My baby had been born into this world on this bed.

Suddenly, the word "born" took on a new and more profound meaning. I realized that Zaeden, that same baby, had yesterday been born into Heaven and into the loving hands of Jesus. Born into Heaven. I liked that. "Born" sounded so much better than "died."

Born seemed a better way to think about it. After all, God had created Zaeden spiritually before he'd ever been placed into his physical body inside of me. Then, 38 weeks later, he'd been born physically into our family. Yesterday, he'd been born spiritually back into Heaven. Yet, I seemed stuck on the physical dying of Zaeden. *Oh Lord, this is so hard to get through! Please help us all!*

# The Power of Pictures

My prayer was interrupted when Grace opened the bedroom door. She saw me lying on the bed, eyes closed in prayer, and quickly expressed apology. Just as quickly she added that she'd found a wonderful toy that meant a lot to her and Zaeden, and could she please give that one to him. The excitement and joy-filled expression in every bit of her body language pulled me from desperate prayer into discussion with her.

Grace's happy face lifted my spirits and body back up to sitting position. We sat and talked about some of the other toys she'd found. She explained dramatically how she'd seen the ping-pong table being filled high with Zaeden's "stuff."

Just as quickly, she got off my bed and left the bedroom. From a sitting position, I could now see around me, but at the first glance around the bedroom, I realized I just wanted to lie down and close my eyes again. The ladies had been in my bedroom, too! *Oh God. This is too much!*

Quickly, I crawled over to my side of the bed where I stashed my books, papers, and stuff. My side of the bed is along the far wall of our bedroom opposite the door, so no one ever looked there. All the kids and even Jim knew that my side of the bed was "my private space" and no one was allowed to get into it! Admittedly, it had been quite some time since I'd cleaned there. I groaned, seeing the organized pile of books, but no dust balls or empty teacups.

Scanning the bedroom, I saw other piles of things had been stacked and straightened as best those ladies could do. There were a few clothes in a pile, but the room seemed in order. That hadn't been the case for many months. I could always justify why some other room needed cleaning more than our bedroom. I just knew this room had to have taken a lot of cleaning to even get to the organized-into-stacks stage of cleaning.

Jim came in to check on me, assuring me that the kids were all fine. I tried to convince him that I was fine as well, but his expression continued to register concern for me. Shortly after he left someone knocked on the door. Dreading having to face anyone, but realizing that I couldn't ignore them, I called out for them to come in. It was my sister, Sandy.

Sandy came into the bedroom, and immediately looked around the room at the stacks and tubs of things. I knew she didn't care that our house was always messy, but the shame was overwhelming. I really wanted to cry, but here in the house, sitting on the bed where Zaeden was born, it seemed inappropriate. This was the room I should be most happy in with wonderful memories of Zaeden. I shouldn't cry, but I wanted to. I wanted to hug Sandy and just cry, but being the older sister I felt that I needed to be strong for her, too.

As if sensing that, Sandy started talking, distracting me with a report on how the kids were all so busy looking around the house and how they'd already found so many of Zaeden's things. She smiled, saying that the kids were keeping the people in our house entertained as they shared stories of having done this and that with Zaeden. While she told me there were many smiles and much laughter, she also had an expression of concern directed at me.

Wanting to divert her attention from me, I scanned the room. Seeing a tub full of pictures near the bed, I got up and pulled the tub toward an open area on the floor and simply sat next to it. I pulled out stacks of envelopes containing developed pictures and negatives and I opened one. Seeing what I was doing, Sandy dug in. Soon, we were looking at the family pictures I'd taken over the past several years, sharing memories of good times.

Sandy asked if other tubs nearby contained photos, too. Yes, they did. She was incredulous of my having taken that many pictures. I had not shared many family pictures with my siblings and Sandy was happy to see them. It seemed almost a gift that she was opening, and I sadly realized that my siblings had not known much of what our family experienced, simply because we lived far enough away that it wasn't feasible to visit each other often.

Another knock on the door and sister-in-law Kristi joined us in sharing stories and looking at pictures. Kristi had closed the door when she entered and I really wanted it to stay closed. It seemed strange, but almost as if the three of us were in our own little world as we sat cross-legged on the floor sharing stories and laughter as the piles of pictures we'd looked at grew ever larger around us.

The majority of pictures were of the kids. They teased me about how many pictures I had taken of this and that and every single event of the kids' lives. I had to admit to them that I was picture crazy. Sitting with a handful of precious pictures in hand, I understood just how priceless those pictures of Zaeden were. Those were the only ones we would ever have of him. *Dearest God, thank you so very much for these gifts.*

By now, several thousand pictures were stacked around us. As we sat looking at each other and all the pictures around us, we all started laughing because I pointed out the several more tubs we had yet to go through. The three of us stopped laughing and looked at each other with excitement. Almost simultaneously, we voiced the idea of pulling out fun pictures of Zaeden and making a collage.

With excitement, we went back through the stacks sitting around us, and pulled out the best and funniest and most expressive favorites. The kids had been putting together a "collage" of Zaeden's toys on the ping-pong table, and now we were doing the same thing with his precious pictures.

It became a mission. Something to do. Some purpose that we could share. Something, anything that could be good for all of us.

Soon we had placed at least a hundred pictures into "Zaeden's" stack.

My youngest sister Julee found the three of us in my bedroom, and joined in the adventure. Every once in a while, one of the kids came into the bedroom and talked about finding something, or reported that this kid had done that to them, or of being hungry, or announcing that someone had come to the house. They'd inevitably join in looking at the pictures, but after several minutes they'd leave the bedroom to venture off to another area of the house.

While I knew that the first floor of the house below my bedroom was noisy with many people coming and going, I felt under no compulsion to leave my bedroom. I didn't want to see anyone, or talk with anyone. Perhaps that was rude, but I just wanted to be in my bedroom, alone with my "sisters." Jim peeked in every now and then, at first concerned about how I was doing, and then accepting of what we were doing. We explained the plan we'd come up with for the pictures, and he lightheartedly remarked that we would probably be in the bedroom for many hours. He was right.

Adriel brought a plate of food into the bedroom for me, but I was so busy talking and looking at pictures, I didn't eat any of it. The food looked good, but I just wasn't hungry. Sandy noticed my not eating and told me that I "needed" to eat. Taking a couple of bites to oblige her concerns, I then put the sandwich down and got back to the pictures.

With four of us digging through the tubs, the conversation swelled to a near-constant buzz. As soon as one of us found an interesting picture, we would exclaim how "cute" or "funny" it looked and the rest of us would stop looking at the pictures in our hands, and scoot closer to that person to look at theirs. Then, there was the telling of the story that went along with that picture, and one of us might remember something else that had happened with another kid in our families similar to that, so that story was shared, as well.

That time became a great story telling adventure. Even more so, it was like a bright and colorful gift that we each got to take turns opening for many hours of that Saturday. Such wonderful memories. Such happy times. With the conversations, we came to understand how each of our families had been blessed. It also seemed we felt blessed to be so close to one another, sitting cross-legged on the floor in my bedroom surrounded by stacks of pictures. The empty feeling I'd felt earlier while lying on my bed was gently fading away, as a strengthening sense of family connectedness became the more important, the better thing, to keep in focus.

The happy conversations and bright smiles in the pictures not only lifted our spirits, but also helped us more easily talk through some of the funeral planning that needed to be done. Every so often, Sandy mentioned a detail here or there that we should plan, or asked a question that needed to be considered. However, when that had been discussed, we all went back to the pictures, changing the subject to happy events we remembered.

So, it was during those next hours that we unknowingly started down the path of making decisions. Every so often, Sandy left the room, and I imagined she carried with her those decisions we'd made and the intention to communicate them with those who needed to know.

As we sorted through the many thousands of pictures, I realized that the majority of the summertime pictures I'd taken had been outdoors, and the majority of wintertime pictures were taken indoors. Several of the pictures I'd just looked through were from the previous summer with the kids playing at our farm. The bright reds and blues, and yellows, and greens in the pictures soon had us all wishful for springtime flowers to brighten up the dull browns and grays of the wintry landscape outside the bedroom window.

Again, it came to mind that Zaeden had always been intrigued by bright colors, and at once I decided that those vivid colors of summertime should be the theme for his church service. Kristi, Julee, and Sandy agreed wholeheartedly.

Scanning through the ever-growing pile of pictures, I saw the kids playing with colorful sandbox toys in the sand pile, or playing ball with each other, or helping me plant flowers around the house. Their smiles seemed to be as bright as the colors of the toys they played with.

Seeing the pictures of the kids planting flowers with me, Sandy asked what florist she could call to order flowers for the service. I told her that I didn't want flowers, because cut flowers always die. Jim had known over the past many years never to give me cut flowers, but evidently my family didn't. When I tried to explain that concept to them, they were at a loss, because cut flowers are normally used for funeral services.

A wonderful idea came to me. I asked Sandy to speak with the florist, and request bright colored pots that contained spring flowering bulbs instead of cut flowers. I told them that after the service I would take them out to our farm and plant a memory garden for Zaeden.

The joy that came with the idea was completely contagious. We talked excitedly about alternatives to flowerpots and instead using perhaps sand buckets, or garden baskets that would be bright reds, and yellows, and blues. Then when Sandy asked what we'd like for a plant, I said I didn't want that, but instead to make a display that would have one of his baby blankets, with a teddy bear and balloons, along with some of his favorite toys. My ideas at this point seemed to stretch beyond what any of us had seen or thought about before, but at the same time it all just made sense!

Sandy and Julee decided to go on a shopping trip to find some bright containers and balloons and spring gardening things. Sandy called the florist, and relayed to us that the florist had become excited about the prospect of fun, beautiful garden displays for Zaeden. We also called a couple of other local florists in case they were asked to provide flower arrangements, and told them the ideas and purpose of our request. It seemed an uplifting sentiment was spreading amongst the four of us and we became eager to see the beautiful, bright garden arrangements that would be placed around Zaeden. We hoped it would be a beautiful tribute and celebration of him.

Every once in a while, some of the kids would sneak into the bedroom and pick up a pile of pictures to look at. Their faces would light up when a particular picture triggered a special memory and they'd blurt out that event, along with details I hadn't known about. It was wonderful to have the kids so interested in helping sort the pictures with us. As the mound of Zaeden's pictures grew to almost toppling over, Kristi and I began to sort through them to pick out the best of those favorites. The pictures began to come together in chunks of time. Pictures of each of the kids holding Zaeden just after he was born. Pictures of friends holding him. Pictures of his baptism. Pictures of him learning to sit up. Pictures of him and Macrae playing together or getting into the kitchen cupboards and making a mess. Pictures of the kids playing outside. Pictures of the older kids helping Zaeden play ball. Pictures of the kids reading to him, etc.

I had not realized how many pictures I'd taken. I tenderly held each picture and easily recalled standing in front of that scene with camera in hand, taking care to snap the picture at just the right time to capture facial expressions or action or with a good background. These were not just pictures. These were carefully chosen, important moments in time.

From the time Taralyn had been born, I'd been a crazy picture-taking mom. Even when Jim bought a video-camcorder, I would not put down my old camera. Even when digital cameras were available, I refused to give up my trusted 35mm film camera. I was so thankful now. Every moment that I had wanted to capture, I had captured. And here, stacked in piles all around, were the pictures to recall those special memories.

I hadn't understood at the time I took those pictures, but I knew now that my mind could never have recalled all the details my camera had captured. If no pictures had been taken, perhaps I could have recalled half of those events, along with some of the details and emotion that were included. But, these pictures allowed me enough recall to expand the memory into the entire event with much more detail and context. Even though each picture captured only a fraction of a second of that event, the picture relayed the expressions, the colors, the room of the house or season of the year, and just by seeing the hairstyles or landscape in the background I could place where and when and whom that event involved. Those pictures unlocked a flood of memories surrounding each of those events.

As the pictures became organized and arranged into a timeline, I secretly wondered if I could pull off getting them placed into a presentation. I did not voice that idea to anyone, because I feared they would think it too ambitious or difficult to complete in time. My mind would not let the idea rest, though. Instead, the idea grew to also making a tri-fold memorial program that contained some of the key events of Zaeden's life to hand out at the funeral.

I understood that the usual types of memorial programs were appropriate for people who had lived long lives and had careers and a history to share. But, we all knew Zaeden as a happy, curious two-year-old, and what was important to him were his family and all the happy times we shared. It just seemed logical to express that by way of pictures rather than words.

The next time Jim came into the bedroom to check on us, I relayed my crazy idea to make a photo presentation. He expressed enthusiasm mixed with skepticism that we could get such a grand feat accomplished. Ignoring his skeptical concern, I used my talk-very-quickly-and-excitedly method in an attempt to sway him. Even as I was saying the rapid-fire words, additional words spilled out. It seemed I was saying the words before I'd even had the thoughts. I asked if he knew where the videotapes were so that we could add some video into the presentation of pictures.

I couldn't believe how those words had come out without my even thinking them beforehand. With relief, I saw Jim's affirmation of this idea, along with an expression of excitement as he left the bedroom. He ran down the stairs and I heard him call out to the kids to come to the living room and help search through tapes to find fun videos of Zaeden.

That request, or rather command, brought footsteps sounding toward him from what seemed like every single room in our three-story home. How wonderful this could be for our family to build a presentation together for Zaeden.

*Lord, please bless this project.*

# A Difficult Decision

By late evening, I was feeling somewhat ready to leave the comfort of my bedroom and brave seeing and perhaps speaking with whomever might be visiting. There was a continual buzz of conversation that could be sourced to every room on the first floor and I wondered whom I might find in our house.

The living room was crowded full with kids of all ages sitting on the couches, the floor, standing in groups, and noisy with various conversations. Taralyn quietly voiced that most of those kids, from her age down, wanted to stay at our house for the night. Even with it being late at night, every level of the house was buzzing with talking and action and eating and doors opening and shutting. I hadn't realized how many people we had in our house, and then I worried whether we'd have enough pillows and blankets for each of them to sleep comfortably.

Our house has always had an open door policy for any of the kids' friends to come in regardless of the time, whether day or night. It was understood that if any of them wanted, or needed, to come to our house they would always be welcome. It was normal to have at least one, or up to five, extra kids staying with us, especially during weekends or when there wasn't any school the next day.

Now, as I meandered my way through the groups of people, I noticed they were content with each other and in discussions of various topics. This was not a time of stiff conversation and crying and I-don't-know-what-I-can-do-to-help. Each of these people seemed to be here because they really wanted to be with us and they knew they were welcome.

I braved my way into the kitchen. I was actually feeling somewhat hungry. As I walked into the kitchen, I saw the table and every counter piled high with food of every imaginable type. Not only that, but the dishes had been kept up with, and someone had been thoughtful in bringing paper plates and disposable silverware.

At once, having seen the relaxed atmosphere in each of the rooms with my kids and all of those visitors and friends and family, and then seeing the clean and welcoming kitchen with all the prepared foods awaiting anyone who was hungry, the previous embarrassment and shame I'd felt of my dirty and disorganized house vanished. It just all vanished.

After I ate, I walked through the rooms around the house and quietly listened in on some of the conversations amongst the kids. They all seemed content and at ease being together. I didn't interrupt that, knowing that they didn't need me.

What surprised me most was the fact that the different ages of kids were mixed together in almost every group. Shaking my head, I smiled and thought it a tribute to how loving and caring my kids' friends had always been to our kids, no matter what their ages. With our house being so small for so many people, it was inevitable that when anyone stayed over, they would continually be interrupted by some of the other ages of kids. Now, it seemed they really wanted that mixing up of groups and continued shuffling from one room of people to the next.

I found Jim and thanked him for being a good host while I'd been hiding in our bedroom. Even though I'd realized long ago that he has obvious talent in greeting and talking with anyone, whether friend or stranger, it seemed this would have been a challenging task even for him. He relayed that, yes, he was very tired, but that he had managed to keep everything running smoothly while I'd been in the bedroom. In sincere thankfulness, I gave him a big hug. With the weak hug I got in return, I understood how weary he was, and we both agreed it was time to try and sleep.

I gathered as many pillows and blankets as I could find and distributed them about the house, then headed back to our bedroom. Jim had already cleared the stacks of pictures from the bed, and showed me where he'd placed them. We both went to sleep immediately.

The next thing I knew, sunlight was streaming through the bedroom windows and Macrae was bouncing on me excitedly saying that someone had just come into the house and was bringing us breakfast. Jim and I scrambled out of bed and stumbled downstairs, finding an assortment of kids still sleeping on the couches, beanbags, and floor of the living room.

We went into the kitchen and saw a vast array of breakfast foods, but the benefactor was nowhere to be found. Macrae could only tell us that the man was big (which usually meant an adult-sized person), with a red shirt, and he was strong because he carried so much food. I realized that we might never know who it was. I told myself that's exactly how I will share a gift of food, too, from now on.

After grabbing some breakfast, I headed upstairs to the bedroom to continue looking through pictures. By late morning, Sandy, Julee, and Kristi had joined me again. Every so often, I came out of the bedroom and walked from room to room checking in on the groups of kids to make sure that they were all okay. I noticed Jim had resumed his hosting duties as he had the day before. I was proud of him for being able to do that. I didn't have the stamina or desire to interact with all those people. It seemed too much. After more than a few minutes downstairs, I'd find myself in quick retreat to the safety of my bedroom.

That afternoon, as Sandy came back in the bedroom after also checking on the kids, she remarked to us that the kids were all getting along so well. Each of us agreed that it was indeed very unusual, but there had not been any major issues that we'd needed to deal with. When Jim came in to check on us later, he confirmed that the kids were all very content and busy with talking and eating and being in the midst of all those visitors.

I realized not one single time had I needed to break up an argument, or settle a disagreement over a TV show or video, or deal with an older sibling telling a younger one to get out of their room. It was amazing how well everybody just got along. Some of the kids worked together to pick up around the house and helped the younger ones get food or read to them to pass some time.

I understood then. I understood why those ladies had come into our house while we'd been at the hospital. It was not to embarrass me or cause me shame. It wasn't just because that was something they could do to help our family. It was because they knew we *needed* them to do that. I clearly saw now that there was no way I and Jim and our kids would have been able to do the cleaning and food preparation. This was the clearest example of Christian love that I had ever received.

With that realization, I didn't feel the need to hide in my bedroom any longer. I quietly left the bedroom and walked down the stairs, taking time to really look at and sincerely greet the people I met as I entered the living room and dining room. As I circled through the kitchen and then back into the dining room, I saw many more people standing pleasantly in groups. Some were eating, some were looking at the mountain of toys and books and stuff on the ping-pong table. Some were getting ready to leave, while others were being welcomed into our house.

I also noticed some laundry baskets of folded, clean clothes stacked up in the dining room. Remembering the empty clothes racks and empty dirty clothes room in the basement, and how ashamed I'd been of that yesterday, I pondered the incredible caring of the ladies who could do such a thing for our family.

Right on cue with my thoughts, I saw Jim opening the door for our friend Eileen. They greeted each other loudly and happily while Jim helped her maneuver a large box of clean clothes through the doorway. As soon as she saw me, she set the box down, rushed to me, and gave me the warmest hug possible. That hug was an incredible gift, and with that, both of us realized no words needed to be said.

I felt the grief in her heart, and as we clung together I felt the connection of my grief meeting with hers. I sensed that she had felt helpless, not being able to do anything to help Zaeden. I thought it strange how all of that was felt in her hug, but I knew it. I truly knew it.

Then I also understood that doing our laundry was something that she could do for us, and that she had not only known it needed to be done, but that she truly wanted to do that for us. She knew what family laundry meant. She and her husband had raised several children. Laundry could be a mess. It could be piled high. But, as I looked into her eyes after that warm hug, I only saw caring and wanting me to know that she would do anything, truly anything, to help us.

How wonderful and awesome were those gifts that the ladies of our community had given our family. They were taking over the cares of our family, so that we could just concentrate on all that needed to be done in the next days. This was completely new to me. I hadn't even known such a thing was done when a death occurs. I wondered why I hadn't been thoughtful to do things such as this when I'd heard of someone experiencing something tragic.

Then, I realized with a new pain in my heart, that some of them must have already experienced a loved one's death. Perhaps they had already experienced the community helping them through that, as we were being helped now. It made sense to showing caring and love for a friend or family member by taking care of household and food needs, but I'd simply not ever experienced that before. I promised myself to be more thoughtful and caring whenever I heard of tragedy in the future.

One of the kids came running over to greet Eileen and we let loose of our hug. Her attention became fixed on conversation with our children. Not only had Eileen been a wonderful friend to Jim and me, but she had always been incredibly caring with all of our children, as well.

I turned to see Jim walking over to me with a haggard expression of "needing-to-tell-me-something." I braced myself, and listened to him explain that we'd need to walk to the cemetery soon and meet with someone to pick out a burial plot. The very words were repulsive to me. I hadn't even considered that needed to be done. But, of course it did. He told me that he'd been out to look through the cemetery earlier in the day, and had found an area that seemed nice and open. He said we were scheduled to meet with someone in a little while and gently asked if I could get ready to go do that.

I physically recoiled at the thought. Then I looked at Jim and saw that he wanted me to go with him to make that decision. Something in his expression called me to look deeper, and I saw that more than anything, he did not want to make that decision alone.

However, more than anything, I did not want to even have to consider such a decision. The decision lay between us, though, and waited. My throat became tight and I tried to swallow so I could speak, but tears tumbled down before I could even make a sound. Breathing hard, I hugged him tight, and we both understood that we'd need to make this decision together in order to get through it at all.

I found a jacket and shoes and then found Jim again and we started the walk together. Jim explained that the person we were scheduled to meet with was Henry. I remembered that he and his wife lived a few blocks from our house and were members of our church. His daughter had died in a car accident many years ago, when she was but a teenager.

I felt nervous, and uncomfortable, and chilled, and wished I could run back into our house. Jim's hand clasped mine strongly, though, and he kept both of us moving forward to meet Henry. We exchanged pleasant greetings, but with sadness mirrored in each other's eyes. Some of Henry's grandchildren attended school with our kids, and although I'd heard about that car accident, I'd never really known much more than that. Henry explained that he still thinks about her and wonders if she would've gotten married, or what career she might've had, or if she'd have had children. I could hardly bear to hear the words, much less gain the composure to speak kind words of comfort in return.

However, as he shared more of her story, we began simple conversation in asking questions, and attentively listened as he relayed more of the story. I'd never been able to get past the tragedy part of hearing a child had died. Now a parent was explaining their experience with it, and I suddenly wanted to hear more. I wanted to know how they got through it, how their other children had done, what it was like for that to have happened so many years ago. Did the pain ever lessen? Did the kids forget about their sister? Did any of them ever talk about it, or was it something that was always too painful to discuss? I didn't dare ask all of those questions, but in listening to Henry talk, I understood the answers in a basic way.

During our conversation we continued walking toward the back of the cemetery, and though the words were difficult for both him to speak and for us to hear, I sensed a bonding pulling our hearts together.

I realized that tragedy does not know time. I saw a father walking beside me who still grieved for his daughter after these many years. After a time of shared silence, Jim asked if Henry would tell us how to choose a plot. By then we'd reached the back, open section of the cemetery. Henry showed us how the plots were laid out and which areas were available, including the area that Jim told me about. As we quietly walked through the adjacent plots we noticed several gravestones for children who'd been buried nearby within recent years.

As we stood in the silence pondering those tragedies and deaths and burials, Henry pointed just a few rows away. With a soft voice, he told us that his daughter was buried there. He also explained that he and his wife had bought the plots next to hers and had already put their gravestone in place for whenever they died. We stood there for quite some time in complete, absolute silence, under a sky as gray and dreary as my heart.

I realized in that silence there was nothing that could be said. Looking at Jim and Henry, I noticed how closely we stood together as a measure of trying to comfort each other. None of us wanted to be there. None of us had wanted our child to die. But, his daughter, Janelle, and our son, Zaeden, had died. As their parents, we needed to be here and make these decisions.

Henry gazed over toward his plots, deep in thought. I knew then I would never forget this day, this minute of standing here and choosing where Jim and I would bury our child. As if in attempt to break the awkward silence, Henry turned to Jim and me with a genuine smile. With almost a laugh, he told us that if we bought the set of plots we were standing next to, we would someday be neighbors. He added, smiling even more brightly, that it would be just great having us as neighbors someday after we'd all died. Jim and I smiled in return and agreed that it would be wonderful to be neighbors. Then he said in a humorous confirmation of our newly realized friendship, that then someday as neighbors perhaps we could play cards together. We simultaneously burst into laughter at this outrageous, but happy thought.

It felt good to laugh. I wanted it to be possible to be happy. I wanted to think of this cemetery not as dismal and under a gray sky, with only gray and reddish brown and black tombstones. In that instant, my perception of cemeteries changed. I understood that Zaeden's spirit was bright and beautiful, and even though his body no longer contained that beauty and brightness, there wasn't any reason to have his plot be a place to cry or avoid.

More than anything now, I wanted to have Zaeden buried right where we were standing. It also seemed wonderful to know that we could be buried someday right next to him. Jim and I looked at each other and knew. We had made the decision that we had only an hour before dreaded so terribly.

Henry looked at us expectantly. Both he and Jim now wore almost comfortable expressions. Jim looked to me expectantly. I smiled and simply shrugged my shoulders.

That sealed the decision. Henry, Mardell, and Janelle and Jim, Zaeden, and I would someday be neighbors, and we could all look forward to playing cards together. Wow! How incredible for this blessing to have been gifted to us. I thanked God for having Henry be the person who helped us with that decision. We'd made a new friend along the way, and strangely a bit of happiness had even resulted. Who would've thought it possible?

# More Decisions

As the three of us walked back toward the front of the cemetery, our steps were lighter. Our conversation lifted as well, and turned to light-hearted discussions of the weather and local events. As we reached the front of the cemetery, though, Henry's expression became somber. Jim and I braced ourselves for his words.

He explained that someone had wanted to donate the money to pay for Zaeden's plot and asked us if we would accept that. That type of gift seemed very unusual to me. I could see by Jim's expression that he was somewhat confused, as well. Henry had already explained that the plots were generally sold as a single plot or a group of four plots, and we'd already chosen to buy four plots.

Looking at each other, Jim and I saw reflected in each other's eyes that this was yet another gift that we needed to accept graciously and not be embarrassed or ashamed about. We told Henry that yes, we sincerely appreciated the gift and would he please relay our thankfulness to the person who wanted to buy Zaeden's plot for us.

With that, we exited the cemetery with a sense of completeness. Shaking hands with Henry now had the touch of friendship, of relief, of it being a goodbye, but that we would be together again. We smiled and waved good-bye to each other knowing that the tough decision here was completed.

As we parted ways, I tugged on Jim's hand to turn and look backward toward the plots we'd chosen. What a beautiful sunrise would be in view from our plots. Yes, I could imagine my body resting in death someday in exactly that space.

Jim and I turned our steps toward home. Holding his hand tight in mine, I gave his an even tighter squeeze. He let loose of my hand and put his arm around me, hugging me close. The decision we'd just made together was monumental. We'd chosen, from this entire huge, wonderful world, our family burial plot.

Knowing that someday my body would be so physically close to Zaeden again was reassuring in a strange, but profound way. It somehow symbolized that we would always be close to Zaeden, even if he were the first to be buried there. That small area of ground now had the Hoflen name written to it and was marked "paid."

Selection of our burial plot gave me a harsh sentencing of my own physical death. A month ago, a year ago, I had not a care about burial plots, or where my body would be placed upon my physical death. What Jim and I had just accomplished had been extremely painful and very sobering. We had needed to acknowledge not only Zaeden's death, but also our own mortality.

Jim and I continued with slow steps toward home. Once inside, a couple of the kids asked us where we'd been. I wasn't prepared for that. It had been hard enough to come to terms with it myself over the past hour. I didn't even know how to verbalize the decision of choosing where to bury Zaeden's body in a way that would make sense to our younger kids.

Jim quickly talked through the basics of a burial plot with them and where it was behind the church. With relief, I saw that they seemed satisfied with his answer.

Turning to walk upstairs, I met Sandy and Julee. Their excited looks had me wondering what they'd been up to, and I was deeply relieved that I didn't have to explain anything about the plot to them. Sandy took over the conversation, saying that she'd found the cutest bear holding onto a vase in one of the stores where they'd shopped. She said she'd gotten it arranged with the florist to have balloons placed in the vase. She then hurriedly asked me to please get the baby blanket and items to put with the rest of the display.

We began rummaging through piles of stuff here and there throughout the house, and luckily found exactly what we'd hoped for. We chose one of the blue baby blankets that Grandma had quilted, along with the white cotton blanket with blue crocheted edging that he'd had when being baptized. Perfect. It was going to be beautiful! Then we went to the ping-pong table and found his brown bear book and a big yellow duck bath toy and a bright blue ball. The kids added this and that to the pile, and we finally had to laugh and tell them enough was enough!

Sandy's arms were piled high. Julee helped her get everything put into sacks to be brought to the florist. Zaeden's treasures were about to be arranged into a bright, beautiful display. A sense of warm peace and happiness spread deep inside me, thinking that Zaeden's spirit would be so happy seeing his special things put together just for him.

Jim met me in the doorway as Sandy and Julee left. He had that same expression of "I-need-to-talk-with-you" that I'd seen earlier. In panic I asked him if something terrible had happened.

I listened with relief, as he explained that, no, nothing terrible had happened. He did need to tell me though, that we needed to meet with the funeral director within the next hour in order to plan some of the arrangements. He further explained that since the drive would take a good twenty minutes, we should leave soon and that Sandy and Julee would meet us there.

I felt as if my body was being tossed back and forth, being told to go here and do this and get that done. We'd just been through making a terribly difficult decision and had tried so hard to make it a good family decision. It had, but I felt that as soon as we'd gained relief in one area, another terrible event stood before us.

The ups and downs of this day began to take their toll. I felt light-headed, and my thoughts became fuzzy. I asked Jim if we could sit down and just talk. The kids were still busy talking and moving in all directions around us, and that suddenly seemed too much for my mind to comprehend. I needed quiet. I needed space. I needed to just be with Jim and have us quietly talk.

We went into the kitchen, where surprisingly it was relatively quiet. Seeing the table of food, I suddenly remembered that I hadn't eaten much the entire day. Jim helped me scoop this and that onto a plate, and put together a quick sandwich. Then as we talked upstairs in the bedroom, he explained again that we would need to leave soon and drive to the funeral home. This time, I could clearly hear him and logically think about what that meant. In between bites of food we discussed a few of the decisions that we thought needed to be made.

I was immensely grateful that Jim had already thought about the things that needed to occur, because I just simply couldn't. I had no idea what needed to be done. I had no idea of where to be when, or with whom, or why. For as long as I could remember, I'd had intense anxiety when thinking about death, especially the possibility of my kids' death.

Telling Jim I'd meet him in five minutes in the van, I brought the half-eaten plate of food to the kitchen and quickly set about the task of finding some things we'd thought of for Zaeden. The kids had pointed out a picture of Zaeden in the special stack of Zaeden pictures. It was a picture of him lying in bed sleeping in his pajamas and holding a red ball. We'd decided we wanted Zaeden to lie exactly like that, just as if he were sleeping.

I showed the picture to some of the kids in the living room, asking if they could help find his pajamas somewhere in the boxes of clean clothes. After a few minutes, one of the kids shouted triumphantly and ran to me holding Zaeden's favorite pajamas. Soon the kids had also found his red ball and pooh blanket.

With all of those precious items gently placed in a bag, I found my coat and told the kids that we would be home in a couple hours. During the drive, Jim and I caught each other up on a few of the things that had been happening. We hadn't had much time alone since getting home from the Rainbow House yesterday.

He had found comfort being amongst the many people who were continuously coming and going through our house. In almost complete opposition to that, I'd needed to stay almost exclusively behind closed doors of our bedroom, and only wanted to see him, the kids, or close family members. The kids had seemed content to float between the openness of the downstairs and finding some respite from the busyness in one of the bedrooms upstairs or in the attic.

It had seemed to me that leaving the kids at the house was best for the planning we needed to do. Jim felt comfortable with that decision, as well. There had been upwards of 40 people at any given time in our house. The kids always had someone starting up a conversation with them, or watching a TV program with them, or asking if they wanted something more to eat or drink. Jim said that with so many people in the house at all times, it was chaotic, but it was also at a busy level that seemed good for the kids.

I suddenly realized that I had no idea what to wear for Zaeden's service. I remembered that the simple black dress I'd worn for my grandmother's funeral several years ago was probably still hanging in my closet. As I thought about wearing that dress, though, I found myself resisting. I didn't want to wear that dress. I didn't want to wear black. I didn't want this to be a "funeral." And I certainly didn't want to dress as if it was one.

Remembering that we'd told the florist to have bright colors and garden toys began a somber thought process. My wardrobe had never included many bright colors. With such a bright colored atmosphere, what would I possibly wear?

I shook my head, sadly realizing that my thoughts about death had been so focused on the death of the body, that I'd never even considered the beauty of spiritual freedom. I'd always linked the black and gray and brown of winter with aging and also with end-of-life and death. That just didn't seem appropriate any more. No, more than that, it didn't even seem true anymore.

I told Jim that I didn't want anyone to wear black to Zaeden's service. He seemed quite taken aback, but as I explained what the florist was putting together and how beautiful the balloons had been, he seemed not only to understand; but he completely embraced this new concept.

We discussed our thoughts regarding the term "funeral" service. I told him of hearing some funerals being called "Celebration of Life" services. Instantly, we agreed Zaeden's would be a "Celebration of Life" service and not a "funeral" service. We discussed and decided that we wanted it to be a celebration of not only Zaeden's physical life; but we also wanted to let everyone know that he was now eternally spiritually alive, and free from his body. Smiling then at each other, I knew that he knew, too. We both knew it was only Zaeden's body that had died.

During that drive, I realized how wonderful it was for Jim and I to talk through those basics. Arriving at the funeral home, we both felt strongly that we could get through the planning details. We'd already agreed that our goal was to make it special for Zaeden. We wanted it to be happy for him. As I watched Jim and noticed the wheels of thought turning in his mind, I knew we would not be planning a typical "funeral" for our beloved Zaeden.

# Rollercoaster Emotions

S cott and Kathie Hockenberry, owners of the funeral home, escorted us to Scott's office and conveyed condolences, kindness, and gentleness. Scott listened to our questions and provided thoughtful explanations. Within minutes, Jim and I looked at each other and I saw with immense relief that we were in complete agreement. We could trust Scott and Kathie to be wonderful caretakers of our family.

When Sandy and Julee joined us, Scott began the decision process with us, explaining each item clearly and simply. He took notes and helped us complete necessary forms. We chose the following evening, Monday, for our pastor and immediate families to have a private time to share with Zaeden. Young adult cousins and friends would be casket bearers; and Tuesday afternoon at 2:00 p.m. the Celebration of Life service would be held at the church. Scott asked if we preferred to have the ladies of the church serve the luncheon after the service, and arrange for the food. Without hesitating, Jim and I said yes.

Finally, a decision that was easy to make! During the past several days, each decision had been so difficult, so overwhelming, and horrible. An odd sense of giddiness washed over me. Being asked an easy question was out of balance with the previously painful and emotional decisions. My emotions swung like a pendulum and I released a raspy laugh. Chastising myself, I forced my focus to stay in somber perspective of the fact that Zaeden had died and we were arranging his service and burial.

With emotions swinging downward again, my throat constricted, and I needed to gulp in a few breaths of air. I felt an overwhelming need to have Zaeden sitting on my lap. I forced my mind to reconcile the close proximity of the room we sat comfortably in being near the room where Zaeden's body lay in death.

Death. That ugly word held me in its grip. How dreadful. How awful. It meant to me an ending. Even worse, it meant a decomposing. I fought the urge to scream. Reaching down to tightly grip my chair, I willed myself to sit still and be silent. With eyes squeezed shut, I tried desperately to imagine holding Zaeden close to me. It was so hard to keep Zaeden's spiritual life in focus, instead of his body's physical death.

I glanced at the others. They were focused on something Scott was saying and seemed oblivious to my rollercoaster emotions.

Scott wrote something in his tablet, and by their nods of agreement it seemed they'd reached a decision that I didn't even recall being discussed.

Taking a deep breath and looking over at Jim with a plea to help me speak, I told Scott that our family was hoping to focus on Zaeden's spirit being alive, and not on the grieving of his body's death. We all relayed our ideas for Zaeden's Celebration of Life service. The words tumbled out of each of us, along with the basic story of our wonder with God's presence and the silver balloon.

Scott's face lit up with a thoughtful, tender smile. He offered to drive his van instead of the more traditional black hearse in bringing Zaeden's body and casket to our church for the Celebration of Life service. I profusely thanked him. In that moment, it seemed we all realized that we'd found the perfect person to care for Zaeden's body. Such a blessing was not a trifle to be quickly dismissed.

Scott showed us catalogs with different styles of caskets. Jim and I were drawn to a plain white casket. Our discussions revved up a notch. We became more of a team with the goal of keeping the black, sorrowful sense of death away from the beautiful light and peace and life of Zaeden's spirit.

I found courage to ask Scott a favor. Smiling, he said he'd do whatever he could for our family. I showed him the picture of Zaeden asleep in his bed lying on his side with a ball in his hand and asked if he could place Zaeden in the casket in pajamas and lying like he was in that picture. Scott nodded thoughtfully, and I knew he understood how much that request meant to us. We handed Scott the bag containing Zaeden's pajamas, blankets and toys, and as we closed the meeting, I hugged Sandy and Julee in thanks for their help, and silently asked God for mercy on all of us within the difficult days ahead.

During the drive home, I shared with Jim that it seemed important for me to speak during Zaeden's Celebration of Life service. Jim voiced concern for me, given how emotional the service would be. I agreed, but said that it seemed God was calling me to speak. After a brief silence, Jim reluctantly agreed.

Back at the house, the continual flow of people in and out was amazing. Mingling amongst them, I attempted to keep conversations light and welcoming. The older kids introduced me to college friends whom I'd heard of but never met. Younger friends laughed and played with our kids, sharing funny memories for a while, and then just playing like kids who aren't burdened with grief.

Late in the evening, the front door had more people leaving than coming in. Kristi and Julee said they were heading back to the motel with their families. They also confided that people in the community had generously donated money toward hotel rooms for family members so they could be here with us. My heart swelled to overflowing. Some had even donated to our local pizza place to help feed them. Such generosity was difficult to comprehend.

The decibel level and numbers of various conversations in the house lowered steadily, until sometime well after midnight, there was at last, silence throughout.

Sighing deeply, I walked quietly into the kitchen, seeing Jim put the last of the food containers into the fridge. With everything having been stilled into slumber for the night, I tiptoed upstairs, glancing into various rooms to check where the younger kids had gone to sleep. A sudden achy tiredness slowed my steps.

I reached the bedroom and heard soft footsteps behind me. Jim's hand gently touched my shoulder and I turned to be welcomed into his embrace. No words were needed, no movements made, no eye contact shared. We simply let the physical comfort in, to the depth of our being, in oneness of grief.

Our younger kids were the first to awaken. Hearing them, I startled into a numb wakeful state. Grief was there upon my waking. I understood then. It was, and would always be, within me. Forever.

This morning, a Monday, was simply another harsh day in our new "forever". What would normally have been a school day and work day for each of the twenty plus people staying in our house, was instead another day we would spend at home sharing time and comfort with each other. We spent most of the day going through photos and videos. That afternoon Jim let me know when it was time to meet with pastor to plan Zaeden's Celebration of Life service.

Sandy and Julee met us there, and we explained to pastor that we wanted a celebration service and not a time of crying and sadness. We described the plans for colorful flower arrangements and wanting to plant a garden for Zaeden later in the spring. We further explained that we didn't want people to wear black, and that we wanted upbeat, uplifting music. We also wanted piano instead of the organ. I requested that we be able to tell the story of what had happened with Zaeden, and the beautiful experience we'd shared with him as he physically died. I also wanted to make a banner for Zaeden similar to the banners we made for the kids when they were baptized, or had their 1$^{st}$ communion, or had been confirmed.

Jim explained that we were not using the normal handouts as provided by funeral homes, but that we were making our own and would have them ready before the service. We also let pastor know that we hoped to have a presentation, and talked through some of the equipment we'd need for that. After the few remaining details were decided, we walked back to the house.

The rest of the afternoon passed in a blur of comforting conversations, directing the kids to find clothes, and relaying information amongst a myriad of people coming and going about our house. All too soon, Sandy was reminding me that we needed to leave soon for the funeral home. Glancing at the clock I saw that it was nearing 6:00 p.m. Adriel and Grace came down the steps leading Blaes and Macrae freshly bathed and dressed. I called out to the kids to gather up the special things they wanted Zaeden to have. Chaos quickly ensued, with this kid claiming rights to a certain toy that another kid had in hand, or stating that someone had "stolen" whatever they had planned to give to Zaeden because they had set it on the ping-pong table Saturday and now it wasn't there. Jim called out to the kids to settle down and just think of what they'd originally chosen and where it could be. The kids became quiet and a few of them went off to different areas of the house.

Fifteen minutes later we had the last of the items rounded up and each of the kids had their precious chosen item in hand. Our family talked over which kids were going to ride with whom, and who could drive what vehicles. This evening had been set aside for only our extended family and pastor to be with Zaeden. I knew the kids would need that time alone with him and without other people being around us.

With the driving arrangements settled, we loaded everyone up and I mentally counted to make sure we were all in the appropriate vehicles. I knew we had to do this, but I truly, honestly didn't want to. *Oh God. How can I help the kids through this?*

Searching for answers the entire way to Atlantic, I arrived at none. The kids were content to hold their toy for Zaeden and talk amongst themselves. I let it be just that. When Jim drove into the city limits I began to explain that when they see Zaeden they might not think he looks the same as when he was alive.

I explained that when our body dies, our heart doesn't pump anymore and our skin isn't warm anymore. I asked them to be careful if they wanted to touch him, but not to be afraid, because Zaeden's spirit was the part of him that was alive yet and he was happy and alive with Jesus. I said that it was just Zaeden's body that we would see, and his spirit wasn't in his body anymore. I told them that Jim and I would be right there with them and that Sandy and Dan and Julee and Greg and Kristi would be, too.

I saw the curious looks on their faces as they got out of the van – looks that said they didn't know what to expect. Jim opened the door for us to go into the funeral home and Scott welcomed us. He led the way for us to see Zaeden. The kids were reluctant to follow us, so I stayed back with them and walked slowly, giving them a pat on the shoulder or squeeze of their hand to encourage them to be strong.

Sandy and Julee and others were already there. We saw at least 50 bright-colored sand buckets and flower pots of beautiful spring flowers and plants completely surrounding Zaeden.

I'd forgotten to even mention that to the kids and it was a huge surprise for them to see all of this around Zaeden. Sandy walked over to the younger kids and took a couple of them by the hand, leading them to see some of the toys mixed in with the flower displays and reading the cards so they would know who sent the flowers.

The older kids walked with slow deliberate steps toward Zaeden. I saw their pained expressions as they saw him. I watched them carefully, and soon went up behind them to give them a hug or squeeze their hands. I had tears in my eyes, too, seeing Zaeden for the first time since I'd had to leave him at the hospital. We all stood there, looking at him in complete silence. Zaeden was lying just as he'd often lain in bed asleep. He was on his side, wearing his favorite jammies, with a ball clutched in his hand.

A couple of the kids moved up closer and put the toy they'd chosen into the casket with him. Soon the older kids were helping the younger ones put their toys with Zaeden, too. Soon Zaeden was surrounded with all of those toys and books and balls and special things they wanted him to have.

The older kids quietly moved to looking at the flowers and reading the cards. For the next half hour, everyone simply mingled with each other. I looked intently at Zaeden's face and saw how vastly different death looks. I didn't know exactly how I expected him to look, but it was not as he now looked lying before me. This was Zaeden, my beloved two-year-old son. Yet, it was not really him. I wanted to touch him, yet I was hesitant. The need to touch him soon overcame my hesitancy, though, and I reached out to caress his face.

Just touching his skin was shocking to me, but I simply had to touch him. This was my baby and I wanted to touch him again. I continued to touch his face and then reached down to touch his hand. Just days before, I'd traced his love from his heart down his hand, then up the hand of each of the kids and further upward to press that love into their heart. Now, Zaeden's heart was no longer beating. I wondered if the kids were still able to feel Zaeden's love in their hearts instead of just seeing Zaeden's body lying in death in front of them.

When the kids seemed to be getting fidgety, I asked pastor to speak with us and say a prayer. After we prayed, they listened intently as he explained the basic order of Zaeden's Celebration of Life service. Pastor also explained that he'd chosen a special song for Zaeden and that we all needed to practice it for the service. He began singing the uplifting words and after repeating the song a couple of times I noticed the younger kids were enjoying the fun melody and the meaning of the words. After the singing, we formed a circle of hands clasped together in shared prayer for safe travels, for God to be with us in the days ahead, and special thanks that Zaeden was now with God and Jesus in Heaven.

# Frenzied Preparations

The ride home was quiet, but every now and again one of the kids would ask a question about the service the next day, or talk about what they'd given Zaeden, or tell us that they'd seen a really pretty flower and pot, etc. Jim and I patiently answered each question, and just let them talk, as they wanted.

When arriving home, the kids' energy came back in full force. Some stayed outside to talk with people who'd come to see us and were waiting outside. Some of the younger kids headed straight for the kitchen, and the rest of us went our separate ways. It was a nice evening outdoors, and soon I found myself carrying a plate of snacks outside to share with our visitors.

Sometime later, Sandy and Julee burst into the house and announced that they'd come up with the idea to put up several of our many pictures into a collage to display during Zaeden's service. My job was to sort through pictures and decide which ones they should use.

Back in the bedroom, I began sorting through the pictures we had found of Zaeden, trying to select the best of the best. Then I saw one of my favorite pictures of Zaeden with Macrae in the bathtub. I sank to the floor with picture in hand and sobbed. I hated this. I hated being alive and knowing my baby had died. I hated having to sort through all of those pictures and seeing such happiness and love, when now all of that was over. He was just two years old! "God," I cried out in desperation, "why did Zaeden have to die? Why?"

I felt a gentle touch on my shoulder, and heard Jim's soft voice as he knelt beside me. At once, we turned together and hugged with a desperation that had me digging my fingernails into his back. I needed to hold him. I needed him to hold me. This was the child we'd created together and we were now bereft of him. My chest was tight against his as I fought both to inhale deeply and then force a deep exhale in between the shuddering sobs. Alone in that bedroom, he and I just cried and cried and clung fiercely to each other.

Many minutes must have passed, but we stayed locked into each other's arms. Neither of us wanted to let go. Neither of us wanted to go through what we knew would be happening the next day. We both knew that before the next 24 hours were over, our precious and youngest son, Zaeden, would be buried into our family's plot of ground in the cemetery just behind the church. *Oh dear Heavenly God, we didn't want that.* We didn't want that to happen with Zaeden. Babies don't belong buried under the ground, I reasoned. They belong in bathtubs, splashing with their bath toys and giggling with their brother, just like the picture I still held.

I heard Sandy's voice downstairs, and with alarm I realized I'd not even gotten a single picture sorted yet. Hearing her footsteps coming up the stairs, Jim and I wiped tears away and let go of each other. I turned back toward the bed just as she entered the bedroom. Calling out to her that I just needed a few more minutes, she hesitated, and it seemed she was taking in the situation of Jim and I needing time to grieve together. She said she'd be back in a few minutes and walked out.

By then Jim had regained composure, and patting me on the back for strength he walked out and down the stairs. I grabbed a washcloth from the bathroom and ran the water until it was as cold as it would get. I covered my face with the wet washcloth, hoping it would jolt me back into focusing on what needed to be done yet tonight. I knew it was going to be a long night. I headed back to the bedroom, looked at the bed and forced myself into super mom mode.

Rifling through one stack after another, I pulled this and that out and went back to this stack and that one and pretty soon had them spread all over, but in my mind I knew exactly what was where. I started picking up pictures from all of those spread over the bed, starting at the foot of the bed. As I reached the last of the pictures lying along the headboard, I heard Sandy's footsteps again on the stairs. As she entered, I pushed the stack of pictures that were in my hand at her and announced that I was done.

She looked surprised, reached out and took the pictures, but then sternly gave me my next task. She said she would be back in a few hours and I needed to have the memorial handout ready by then. As she walked toward the door, she added that when I was done with it I needed to put it on a CD and that she and her son Dion would then drive to a 24 hour print shop in Omaha to have them printed. I began to protest, and she called out to me that she didn't want to hear it and that I just better have the handout ready and on the CD in a couple of hours.

I had no choice. Grabbing my laptop, I hopped onto the bed and plugged in and powered it up. Jim came in the door and asked if I was doing okay. The tenderness in his eyes calmed my anxiety. I smiled as best I could and assured him that I was doing okay now. I not only saw, but also truly felt, the love flowing between us, strengthening me and warming my heart with peaceful acceptance. I knew that our love would get us through the next 24 hours. I also knew that we could draw on that love for the strength to help our kids and other family members and friends tomorrow.

Jim held a CD in his hands. He said that while we'd been to see Zaeden earlier in the evening Taralyn's friends had worked at high speed to finish scanning all the pictures I'd had on my bed, and that he'd put them onto the CD for me to put into the handout. Incredulously, I stammered a thank you, and wondered how in the world they could have accomplished that without my knowing it. Jim smiled, and I saw that he had wanted to surprise me with this gift from him and the kids' friends.

My thoughts whirled at top speed thinking of what I could now do with the handout. Jim said he was going to get to work on the slide presentation, and that he thought he had some software that could help him get some video put in, as well. With excitement, I took the CD from his outstretched hand, and slid it into the laptop. I would use the announcement I had done for Schuyler's graduation as a template for this handout.

I selected pictures from the CD, re-sized them, placed them in order, made labels, and spaced them on the handout. Midway through this, out of the corner of my eye, I saw Sandy come in. She asked with only the tiniest bit of hope whether I was done yet? Without looking at her, I said that I was happy with how it was turning out, and that it would be done in perhaps a half hour. In reply, Sandy simply stretched out on the bed. Glancing just beyond my monitor, I saw how extremely tired she looked, and as she closed her eyes, I told her to go to sleep and I would let her know when I was done.

By now it was well after midnight. Time seemed to be void of meaning, and I just let my mind focus on the task in front of me. Jim came upstairs to check on me once and tell me that the kids, plus several others, were all accounted for, and that they'd all finally settled down into sleep. He didn't even know some of the kids that were spending the night, but we knew they wanted to be with our family, so we just let it be.

He excitedly told me that he'd figured out how to incorporate Zaeden's baptism video into the presentation, as well as Grace's singing that would play while the pictures displayed one after the other. He asked how the handout was going and I told him it would be done pretty soon, and then I would help him with the presentation. He wondered what order we should put the pictures in for the presentation. I said that we just needed to get them in anywhere. He looked relieved at that loosening up of my normal perfectionism, and went back downstairs to continue his project.

About 4:30 in the morning, I finally had the handout finished. I copied it onto a CD and was about to take it downstairs to drive it to Omaha when Sandy woke up. She was dismayed that I'd let her sleep that long, and frantic that she wouldn't get it printed in time. I told her that I'd already called the print shop and that they were waiting for it. We argued about who should take it, but she said Dion would drive. Without another word, she ran out the door with CD in hand.

Several hours later, as the last picture was placed into the slide presentation and grouped with the audios and videos, Jim and I hugged each other with astonished satisfaction. As the file processed into being saved and copied onto a DVD, he started up yet another pot of coffee and I heated up water for yet another cup of tea. The clock read 8:00 a.m. as Jim slipped the DVD into our television. All of the sorting of pictures and finding of videotapes and audiotapes and organizing and scanning and downloading software and everything that needed to be done was in fact done. Reaching out my hand to grab hold of his, we steadied each other, braced for disappointment. The chances were slim-to-none that our precious videos, audios, and photos had been being successfully merged into video. Neither Jim nor I had ever attempted that complexity before. We stared in complete silence at the TV and waited. I didn't dare breathe. I didn't dare hope.

The sudden burst of video onto the TV screen was simultaneously alarming and thrilling. *Glory hallelujah! God how awesome You are!* Grabbing hold of each other in a victory hug, we silently danced with joy right in front of the TV with those several kids still sleeping around us!

As if on cue, Sandy came in the front door. She bore the look of triumph, handing me a paper sack with several hundred copies of Zaeden's handout. As Jim and I reached out to include her in our victory hug, she noticed the video playing. She shot one of her stern "I-know-you-didn't-get-any-sleep looks," but then shook her head and smiled in approval. We watched a bit of the presentation and then she showed me how wonderful the handouts turned out. She directed me to have some of the older kids fold the handouts properly and bring them to the church by noon. Glancing backward at us as she left, Sandy called out that she was going to the motel to get the rest of the family up and going for the day. Jim went back to the computer to make a back-up DVD.

By now, kids all throughout the house were awakening from their sleep. As one or two of them stumbled down the stairs, another one or two would wake up in the living room. After helping the little ones get to the kitchen and find some breakfast, I realized it was time for my next project. Calling out to Jim that we'd already laid out the kids' clothes the night before, I ran out the door, and sprinted over to the church and down the stairs to my Sunday school classroom.

I found the banner supplies just as unorganized as I knew they would be. Rummaging through several boxes and tubs, I found my scissors, hot glue gun, iron, white felt, silver braid and cord, dowel, ultra heat-n-bond sticky stuff, etc. Next, I looked for the special fabrics that would be perfect for Zaeden's banner. Grabbing a handful of shiny primary color fabrics and a rough textured brown fabric, as well as a bright, shiny silvery material for the lettering, I spread them over the table and got to work. Just then, I heard footsteps and voices overhead.

In exasperation, I remembered I was still wearing a nightshirt and sweat pants, hadn't showered in three days, and my hair and face most assuredly betrayed my sleep and sanity-deprived status! Promptly changing plans, I stuffed all the supplies into a plastic bag. I quietly closed my Sunday school room door, tiptoed up the stairs, and made a mad dash out of the church and back to our house. Not only did I not want anyone to see me, but also I simply couldn't be interrupted, or I'd never get the project done in time.

The only open hard surface space I found available at home for working on my project was the living room floor, which was now unoccupied of sleeping kids. I tossed blankets and pillows out of the way, spread out the bag of supplies, and called out loudly to all household persons thereby declaring that space an official "for-project-use-only" zone. That meant that anyone was welcome to help or ask questions about making the banner or watch, but that I was off-limits and had no time or tolerance for settling the kids' arguments, or finding lost items, etc. Measuring the felt for banners, cutting material, tracing letters and ironing sticky stuff to them was something I could go into automatic mode on because I'd helped in the making of hundreds of banners over the past eighteen years.

The kids had been watching all around me as I cut and ironed and glued, but they were respectfully quiet in letting me work on the banner. A couple of the older kids and adults helped with the cutting of letters and assembling of materials, and before we knew it, the pieces were ironed and glued into place.

As I tied the silver cord onto the dowel that supported the banner, I swung the banner upward and in front of me. The sunlight coming in the living room window danced off the shiny materials that seemed to be twinkling at me. How awesome! The banner had Zaeden's name and the date of his Celebration of Life service in the shiny silvery material, and the center of the banner displayed a fuzzy brown bear holding onto blue, red, and yellow heart-shaped balloons.

Now, seeing me hold it up in the sunshine, the kids giggled with delight at how cute it looked. All that was left was to paint the words "We Love You Zaedy Bear" when I got it to the church. I didn't dare do the painting at the house, because it was windy outside, and I didn't want the paint to become smudged while carrying it from the house to the church.

As a finishing touch, the kids chose sparkly jewels to add to each balloon, and then together we declared Zaeden's banner ready to take to the church. Jim simply smiled at the group of us and then with raised eyebrows directed me to look at the clock. Oh dear. It was already 10:00 a.m.

I asked the kids for the status on them getting dressed for the day and who needed yet to be bathed. Surprisingly, they seemed on track for time, and Taralyn assured me she would help with what was left. That left me with getting bathed and dressed before I would even dare to go to the church again. Rummaging through boxes of clean folded clothes that the ladies had brought back to our house, I managed to find a towel, washcloth, and underwear.

I dashed upstairs, and started running water into the bathtub. I had a couple minutes while it filled to find something to wear, but I couldn't even think what that could be. I'd already undressed, but peeked out the hallway door anyway, and seeing no one, I dashed into my bedroom. Mortified, I saw that someone was in the bedroom, but with relief I realized it was Jim.

What was I thinking to have just run around the house with no clothes on? Looking at me in astonishment, Jim walked into the bathroom and grabbed a towel, saying that I might need that. I stammered that I was just trying to quickly find something to wear while the bathwater was running, but he simply shook his head and left the bedroom, carrying the shoes that I supposed he'd been looking for before I dashed in.

*Dear God, I am delirious from the events of this past week, and not having slept much and not eaten much. How in the world am I going to pull myself together enough to speak to all those people during Zaeden's service?* During the pleading praying time with God, I had begun to scan the items hanging in my closet. *I am not going to wear black. I know You want all of us to be happy for Zaeden's spirit and not mourning for his body.*

Thinking about the colors that Zaeden liked best I saw a bright blue dress. Tugging it out of the closet, I inspected it. I hadn't worn that dress since last summer. It had some wrinkles, but maybe after I'd worn it for a few hours they would straighten out? It somehow seemed to be just the right thing to wear. It was a longer length, and I remembered then that probably every pair of my panty hose had runs, and if the dress were longer, perhaps people wouldn't notice so much.

It was already going on 11:00 a.m. I wouldn't have time to drive the 15 minutes it would take to get to the nearest store and buy a new pair of panty hose. I wondered why in the world I hadn't decided what I would wear yesterday, when I would have been able to iron the dress, or perhaps even wash it! I could've gotten a new pair of panty hose and spared myself certain embarrassment today. Opening the drawer, I realized the truly sad state of my panty hose.

In all my years of being a "woman" I never had enjoyed being dressed up. It wasn't me. I stopped rummaging through the drawer, realizing at that very instant how much I resented having to be anything but who I really was. And the strongest calling I'd ever felt was simply to be a mom. That's what I was comfortable being. That's who I really am. *Does any of this make sense, Lord?*

No reply. Not that I expected any, but I had started talking with God frequently now. Since I'd felt His presence in the hospital, it seemed I was so close to Him that everything on my mind could be okay to talk with Him about or question Him about.

Turning my attention back to my drawer of under-things, I spied one last pair of hose. Hastily searching each leg to inspect it for runs, I discovered to my delight that the only run was in the big toe of the left foot. Maybe if I put enough nail polish on the run, it wouldn't get any larger. As I grabbed up that pair of hose and the dress, I realized I'd forgotten completely about the water running in the tub! What if the water was overflowing?

Why had I taken so much time in the bedroom looking for clothes to wear? Peeking out into the hallway and luckily seeing no one, I dashed into the bathroom with towel, pantyhose, and dress in hand. The bath water was just high enough for a good hot soak, although I certainly didn't have time for that. A knock at the door sent me diving for cover under the bubbles. With relief, I heard Macrae begging to come in to use the bathroom. I said okay, of course. Shaking my head as I scrubbed shampoo into my hair, I wondered how it could possibly be that any of our kids aged five years and younger would always need to use the bathroom at the exact time I was in the bathtub? It seemed to be one of those strange laws of motherhood, and over the years I'd honestly marveled at the darned-near one hundred percent track record the kids had on interrupting my bath time.

Seeing the bubbles in the bathroom distracted Macrae and he ran right over to the bathtub to scoop out a big handful. Blowing into his hand, he sent several globs of bubbles airborne and giggled with delight. Looking again at the bathwater, his face relayed concern. "Mommy," he said, "you always put toys in my bath. You need toys, too!" I hurriedly tried to reason with him that no, I didn't really need bath toys, but as I rinsed the shampoo out of my hair, I felt the splish-splash of toys being tossed into the bubbles around me.

Macrae was beaming a huge smile of satisfaction at me. I didn't have the heart to take the toys out of the water. I just couldn't. But, I did tell him thank you, and asked how did he know that those toys were my favorites? He looked at me with the most curious of looks, and then in a no non-sense voice he told me that I needed to play with the toys. Picking up a yellow duck I promised I would, and with that, Macrae turned and ran out of the bathroom, evidently forgetting what he had originally came into the bathroom for.

The yellow duck still in hand, I understood that Macrae probably hadn't needed to use the bathroom at all. He just needed to have some time with me and wanted me to be happy. Looking at the bright colored bath toys floating around me amongst the bubbles, I couldn't help but smile. I actually felt decades younger, and setting the yellow duck into the bubbles, I blew across the water. The yellow duck bobbed toward Nemo, the fish, and as they bumped up against each other, I giggled at how funny it all looked.

Here I was, forty-some years old, sitting amongst a tub full of bubbles and bath toys. Honestly, it felt exhilarating. As I scrubbed myself clean the toys gaily bobbed around me. The colors and shapes became a game of identifying what toy was where. Instinctively, I grabbed the little yellow ducks and set them down in the bubbles next to the big yellow duck. But, soon I noticed that the little ducks were floating hither and yon mixing in with the blue and red boats and the brown cow and purple dolphin.

Even as I finished rinsing the conditioner out of my hair, I felt lightness and tingling that was only describable as the purest of joy. Even as I toweled dry, that awesome joy resonated through me. I found myself humming as I dressed; and when I looked in the mirror to finish putting on make-up, I noticed I was smiling.

The blue dress seemed to perfectly match the twinkling in my eyes. I never wanted to lose that feeling. This was a special day just for Zaeden and I was happy. *Lord God, thank you for helping this be a special, happy day for Zaeden.*

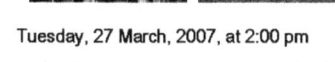 Tuesday, 27 March, 2007, at 2:00 pm
At the Elk Horn Lutheran Church, with visitation prior to the service

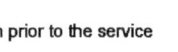 Arrangements by Hockenberry Funeral Service, Atlantic, IA

## *Celebration of Life*

I finished brushing my hair and went back to the bedroom to search for shoes. Along the way, Grace met me and said that she was almost ready, and that the rest of the kids were, too. I dragged several pairs of shoes out from under the bed and found a sensible pair of dark blue shoes. I raced downstairs. As I reached the bottom of the staircase, I looked down at my feet and saw that the run in my panty hose had started up the back of my left leg. Oh no! I'd forgotten to use nail polish. Dashing back upstairs, I grabbed nail polish and lathered on a good layer around the hole and along the run up the back of my leg. I chastised myself for forgetting, but I simply didn't have time to change panty hose at this point. Besides, did I even have a pair in better condition?

Dashing back downstairs, I saw that it was well after 12 o'clock. The service would start at two and I didn't even have the words painted on Zaeden's banner. Seeing that the girls were ready to go to the church, I asked if they could help me with the banner.

At the church, we went downstairs to my Sunday school classroom. They helped me pick out colors for each word: "We" purple, "Love" red, "You" Blue, "Zaedy" yellow, "Bear" green.

When it was done, we held it up and smiled at how cute and bright it looked. I asked them to carry it upstairs and to find Dad so he could help them hang it up. They raced off, carrying the banner with wet paint as carefully as they could.

Sitting down in a chair, I breathed a sigh of relief. Adriel had told me while I was painting the words that Jim had the little guys with him, and the older kids were now at the church as well. Now, I could take a minute or two and try to re-group. I heard more and more footsteps overhead. The church staff had told me yesterday they were planning on at least 200 to 300 people at the service. It sounded as if half of those people were now milling about above me.

With alarm I realized I'd not even written out what I would say during the service. I grabbed a notebook and pen. What could I say that would be meaningful? I could start out with a bit of history about our family and Zaeden. I could then talk about how special Zaeden's birth was and how much joy he'd always brought to us.

I started scrawling words onto paper. One sentence after another tumbled out and landed into paragraph after paragraph. When I'd written about a page worth of words, I stopped to re-read. Oh dear! Slashing out words and writing better ones soon made a mess on the paper. Looking at my watch I saw that it was nearly one o'clock. Oh, no! I should be with my family!

I panicked, tore out a clean page and started writing again. In a few minutes, that page was full. Looking at my watch again, I tore out a third piece of paper and was madly scratching down words, when I heard the classroom door opening. Sandy looked at me sternly, like she'd been looking for me, now had found me, and certainly wasn't very happy with me.

When she sat down beside me her expression softened as she glanced at the scrawling on the pages in front of me. She gently asked me what I was going to talk about during the service. I launched into reading the pages, but they were so messy that I stumbled through most of it. She put her hand on mine, lowered the pages, and said, "Lori, stop."

I looked at her with frightened eyes. She softly told me that I didn't need to write down what I was going to say. That I already knew what was important to say, and I just needed to speak about Zaeden from my heart.

I began to relax -- quieting my thoughts and just feeling my love for Zaeden. The overwhelming joy I'd felt while in the bathtub of toys was let loose again inside of me, and I could see in my mind the cute picture of Zaeden and Macrae playing in the bathtub with their toys. Sighing a huge, deep long sigh, I smiled at Sandy. She was right, of course.

Julee walked into the Sunday school classroom then and Sandy asked me what I would like her and Julee to say. As we talked it through, we decided it would be best for the three of us to walk up together in support of each other. I could talk about the main part of Zaeden's story, and Sandy could explain how the kids and family and friends went outside the hospital and waited to release the balloons. Then, Julee could explain that some of them had seen the silver balloon floating above the hospital and how special it felt when they released the balloons.

With that plan, Sandy pulled me to my feet and told me she wanted to show me what she and Julee and Kristi had done with all those pictures of Zaeden. I'd forgotten about that, but as she led me into the dining room, I saw a long row of tables set up to display the 2' x 4' frames of Zaeden's pictures. I clapped my hands over my mouth, not even knowing what to say, but simply not able to take my eyes off the breathtaking display. Each of the frames had many pictures displayed, each picture bordered by bright cardstock. Several of them had foam letters spelling out cute words to accompany the pictures.

Sandy explained that they had been up very late in the night getting all six of the frames finished, and they were so excited for me to see it. Every picture in those frames was beautiful, and as I gazed from one to the next, I clearly saw the spirit of joy that I felt deep inside of me connecting with the spirit of joy in Zaeden's eyes! That bright, colorful spirit of joy was what I'd felt in the bathtub that very morning and was the very same spirit of joy I now saw in so many of the pictures of Zaeden.

I could not take my eyes off of the display of his pictures. I had taken each of those pictures and as I looked from one to the next, I was gifted not only with a sharp memory recall of the event but also focusing in on seeing Zaeden spiritually for the first time ever. Ever since coming home from the Rainbow House and seeing each of the kids spiritually, I'd tried to look at other family members, the kids' friends, and visitors to see them spiritually also. It was somewhat difficult because I'd always been so focused on the physical aspect of people. Now, a huge blessing was being given to me; I was able to go back in time through the pictures of Zaeden and truly see him spiritually. Wow.

As Julee and Kristi and Greg joined us at the display table, I hugged each of them with tears of thankfulness. Looking somewhat embarrassed at my exuberant reaction, they tried to make their project seem like it was no big deal, saying it was something they wanted to do for Zaeden. *Oh God, thank you for the gift of seeing Zaeden not only physically, but also spiritually through these pictures. Please bless each person that helped put together this picture display.*

Jim came downstairs to find me. We walked upstairs together holding hands and stood in front of the casket to look at Zaeden. His closed eyes and pale skin were in such contrast to all the spirit-filled pictures I'd just seen of him on the display table. With stark realization, I again clearly saw that this simply was not Zaeden. It was Zaeden's body, yes. But, it was not Zaeden. That body had died, and Zaeden's spirit had been freed.

Jim let go of my hand and put his arm around me. We stood close to Zaeden for a long while in quiet thought. I straightened a few of the toys surrounding him and touched him tenderly.

Every so often a couple of the kids would come over to us, wanting to see Zaeden again. After a time, Jim and I looked at each other and simultaneously we both knew. It was time.

I gently called out to the kids who had gathered into groups nearby. All of us walked together into a large side room where pastor was waiting. As we were being seated, Scott came quietly over to Jim and me and led us back to see Zaeden again. Scott gently told us to take whatever time we needed.

Staring down at Zaeden, I looked deeply at him, so that I would never, ever forget that moment. Stroking his soft hair, I told him how much we loved him and Jim told him how thankful we were to have him for a son. I looked at each of the things that the kids had chosen to place beside him. Above him, I saw the white cloth with teddy bear and balloons that Sandy had embroidered in bright colors. It looked beautiful and the words "We love you Zaedy

Bear" preciously expressed our feelings. Yes, I loved my son, Zaeden. I dearly, deeply loved him. I would have rather died than him.

Standing beside me, Jim seemed to be experiencing those same emotions. Holding each other tightly, we stood and looked at Zaeden and caressed him lovingly. In desperation, I fought the instinct to cry out with the pain that rose up from deep within me. This was my precious two-year-old son!

Still touching Zaeden's hand, I felt a strengthening. I looked at his face and then at the gifts that the kids had lovingly placed beside him. Each of us had placed an item of this world beside his body that was also of this world. It was nearing the time when we needed to say goodbye to that physical part of Zaeden. At that instant, I realized that the knowledge and gifts that I'd been blessed with over the past several days were not intended for just me, but for everyone in this world who wanted to hear Zaeden's story.

I knew I must keep hold of the spiritual strength I now felt as I physically touched Zaeden's hand. Then, something called out to me to let go of his hand, and I automatically did so. My hand had left his, but the deep spiritual connection remained. I knew it was time to let go of Zaeden's body. His body had been lovingly cared for and had many loving items placed around him. His body was surrounded with love and always would be. It was okay for me to let go.

*I am releasing his physical body to Your care now, Lord.*

I grabbed hold of Jim's hand. Without saying a word, we kept tight hold of each other, and walked back to the side room where the rest of our family waited.

As we walked in, I smiled toward the kids and sat down amongst them. Pastor had started talking with them about the service. He explained that in a little while we'd all walk out of this room and follow Zaeden into the church. He said he would lead us playing the guitar and it was our job to sing the song we'd sung last night loud and clear because we'd be teaching that song to everyone else in the church.

He explained that then he would welcome everyone and say a prayer, and then I would speak. Jim would speak next, and Greg and Kristi would read the poem we'd selected for the handout. We'd sing "Jesus Loves You" next and after a few more words from him and another prayer the service would be done. He explained after that we would follow Zaeden out of the sanctuary and we'd have some more prayer time outside with him.

Everyone sat in somber and an all-too-awkward stillness. Quickly picking up his guitar, pastor said that we should again practice the song we would be singing as we walked into the sanctuary. The boisterous strumming of the guitar seemed to startle each of us. As he began loudly singing the words, although some mouths were moving, their words were hardly more than a whisper. Being more of a follower than leader in singing, I found my own voice lacking, too, as I shakily tried to squeak out some words.

It seemed that everyone in the room was consumed with the physical death of Zaeden, and none of them showed the joy or peace of knowing God's presence with us in that very room.

I simply had to shake loose the sadness smothering the joy of the song. Turning toward everyone, I started singing out the words loudly and with gusto. Jim and our little kids followed suit, and measure-by-measure the confidence and sound increased as we sang, "Be Bold. Be Strong. For the Lord Our God is With Us." The song's words reinforced what we were to feel and then sing even more loudly and confidently. Yes, we needed to be bold to get through this service. Yes, we also needed to be strong. *Lord, please gift everyone at this service with Your presence of peace and joy so they can be open to hearing what Zaeden's story is really about.*

The quick tempo of the music, and the strength of individual voices surrounding our family, lifted the burden of grief and gently carried our family step-by-step toward the front of the sanctuary. As he reached the front pew, pastor moved off to the side, still strumming the guitar. He turned to face the congregation, his strong voice now booming directly toward us. As pastor had moved off to the side, the front of the sanctuary came into full view before me. A brilliant rainbow of floral colors radiantly adorned the pure white casket. The centerpiece was breathtaking, with the teddy bear centered amongst vivid colors of toys and balloons. I stared, mesmerized at the sight of Zaeden's casket, so small, and so lovingly cradled within the bright colors that he so loved.

As the guitar's last chord faded, and with individual voices quieting all around, an air of expectation floated toward the front of the sanctuary. Pastor welcomed everyone to Zaeden's Celebration of Life service and invited us to be seated.

He addressed the congregation with scripture and prayer. His words seemed distant, and only a portion of them distinct enough to comprehend, as my eyes focused on the colorful splendor before me. Tears blurred the rainbow into bursts of color-filled stars. The white casket in the center became beams of brightness completely filling the front of the sanctuary. In that instant I saw my child securely cradled in Heaven's radiance of color and light.

Zaeden was now experiencing life, even more so than when he had been alive in his body. His life was now a brilliant spiritual life.

Pastor's scripture reading ended, and I tried to focus on the world around me once again. I felt a hand on my shoulder and heard pastor's voice transition into the next part of Zaeden's service. Instinctively, I knew it to be Jim's touch on my shoulder, and felt transference of strength flowing from him into me. Closing my eyes, I attempted to gain composure and confidence for what I knew lay before me.

Jim withdrew his hand from my shoulder and sudden panic set in. Pastor was looking expectantly at me, motioning for me to come forward to the lectern. I stood upright, but my knees felt wooden as I tried to step forward toward the altar. Sandy and Julee appeared alongside me, and we stepped carefully amongst the rainbow of floral color to the lectern. Pastor took a seat behind me, and Sandy and Julee stood in close accompaniment to my right. I was amazed. The church was filled to overflowing.

Glancing again across the vast congregation assembled before me, I realized my lack of a written script left me with no choice. I prayed with all my heart. *Please, God, have mercy. Flow through me and help all those before me be open to hear of Your awesome power and gracious presence through the unfolding of Zaeden's story.*

I sighed heavily, and smiled embarrassingly, then confessed that I had never spoken to such a large group before and did not consider myself a good speaker. I added, though, that I stood before them with confidence and conviction in my heart that Zaeden's story needed to be told and I hoped that they would enjoy Zaeden's Celebration of Life service.

The entire congregation was completely silent, as if all were holding their breath, waiting for something. I, too, was silent and in anticipation. Then, something altogether mysterious and magical happened. Something awesome came into me and surrounded me gently and sweetly. I recognized it. God's mighty presence was there for all to bear witness to in that sanctuary.

My words began to flow, but I knew not the order or of what structure. They just flowed. The words poured freely and clearly from front to back of the sanctuary and up into the balcony. As it had been in the hospital room when Zaeden's spirit left his body, the presence of God was thick, tangible, and powerful.

I relaxed in that awesome peace and comfort of being cradled within the loving arms of Jesus. An additional sensation, though, heightened my wonder and awe of that presence. It was not only around and within me; but that holy presence was also powerfully flowing outward from me. My words were clearly from, and of, God.

I just let it happen. I let the words and message pour freely. My mind seemed disconnected from the river of words and accompanying body language. No thoughts were necessary. My brain was not formulating the sentences. I was completely captivated by this incredibly humbling experience of giving my "self" to be of service to God.

Now able to see the individual faces in the crowd and their reactions to the outpouring of Zaeden's story, I gained the insight of the worth, the priceless value, of each person seated before me in that sanctuary. I no longer saw the persons seated before me as simply a "congregation" of people.

I saw each as a precious person that God had created in His own holy image, holding out His hand for each of them to keep hold of.

I saw each as a dearly beloved person that Jesus had sacrificed His life for, pouring out His holy and precious blood for each of them to receive and be in communion with.

I saw each as a unique person that the Holy Spirit had blessed with special gifts, and wanting to bestow even more blessings to.

I felt honored and humbled to stand before each of them in the sharing of Zaeden's story. The divine indwelling that by now had become comfortable within me had transformed me from the inside out. As the words continued to pour freely, I literally felt as if my spiritual essence, the very core of my being, was now open and exposed for all to see. Along with that, my beliefs and values and understanding of my purpose in this world had also been turned inside out. My spirit was powerfully in union with God and I now felt treasured, precious, and beloved as His child. I had been accepted by Him, even though I had made many mistakes and did not deserve His forgiveness. I felt protected and I did not fear death anymore.

With deep conviction I said that religious "hope" was something that I long ago embraced and "faith" was something that I was uplifted into during the last day of Zaeden's physical life. But in those last moments of Zaeden's physical life, God had gifted me with His presence, "knowing" that He is real, "knowing" that He cares for each of us as He does for Zaeden, and "knowing" also the gifts of mercy, compassion, and grace that He was now offering as gifts to each of us.

I remember that at some point in my speech, I gave special thanks to the personnel in our rescue squad for how professional and caring they'd been, as well as to the hospitals for doing all they could to help Zaeden. I finished speaking with a deep sense of fulfillment.

Walking back to where our family was seated, I looked for Jim, and saw him smiling with pride at me, tears streaming down his face. Gently helping me sit next to him, he put his arm around my shoulder, and hugged me tightly. Looking toward the now empty podium, I thought about what my message had been and how the words had seemed clear and orderly. Now, though, only a minute or two after speaking them, I could not recall the specific words. Only basic topics came to me, and that I had shared Zaeden's story during that timeframe.

Panic struck and my hug tightened with Jim. Sensing my anxiety, he lifted my chin to look him straight in the eyes. I saw strength relayed to me in his eyes, but also pleading. Immediately we both knew that I needed to pull myself together because it would take both of us being strong to help our children and everyone else through this ceremony.

Jim came forward with sincere, emotional gratitude for all those who were present and all those who had provided food and shared time with our family during this difficult time. He gave special thanks to our kids' friends who had dropped everything in their busy lives to spend these past several days with our family.

Sandy and Julee spoke of this special family time together. Greg and Kristi read the poem we had selected; we sang *Jesus Loves You* to Zaeden; and it was time for the slide show and music presentation that we'd just finished at sunrise that morning.

Great joy mingled with overwhelming grief as Jim and I, now seated again, held hands tightly, focusing intently on each slide. None of our kids, nor the rest of the family, had seen the video before the service, and now all eyes were directed attentively on the screen. Both laughter and tear-filled emotions resonated around me.

The photos moved from one to the next, and my tears flowed heavily as I allowed myself to remember and enjoy all of those special times our family had experienced together while Zaeden still lived physically.

I remembered the story of Lazarus' death and how Jesus had openly wept amongst his sisters, Mary and Martha, and friends as they walked to Lazarus' tomb. I felt a tugging at my heart and the compassion of Jesus holding me closely, saying that it was okay to weep, to cry, to grieve Zaeden's physical death. Jesus truly understands. But, He also died on a cross for us so that, even during the harsh and cruel tragic events of our lifetime in this world we would know that death is not the ending. I pressed my hand close to my heart and felt the presence of Jesus within me, and knowing that as He was holding me so close He was also cradling Zaeden in His arms. That blessing of comfort, though, had my tears flowing even more, but this time I simply let them pour out of me freely.

Jim released a river of tears, as well, and I prayed that God would comfort each of us as our family grieved for our beloved Zaeden. Glancing at our kids seated all around us, I saw their tears converge with happy memories brought to mind from the photos and video. Looking more closely, I also saw a depth of thought and wonder that I hadn't seen before the service. I prayed that God would help them see beyond Zaeden's physical death to focus instead on the bright rainbow of blessings within Zaeden's spiritual life.

The magnitude of peace, and floating sensation of God's love, lifted me into a standing position as Zaeden's Celebration of Life service ended. Several of the cousins and our older children's friends carried the casket down the aisle, leading pastor and our family out of the sanctuary singing, "Be Bold, Be Strong, for the Lord our God is With Us."

# Epilogue

In the second book of this series, my family and I take the next big steps in our journey. I invite you into the timeframe where the caring people who brought meals to our home return back to their normal lives, yet we can never return to what had been normal for our family. Within the depths of isolation and loneliness, I desperately long for a hug or touch from Zaeden. Setting the table with one less plate and finding yet another sweater that was Zaeden's in the laundry room torment me so deeply that I find myself immediately crying uncontrollably.

In the midst of battling that huge, dark emptiness and agony, I dare to scream questions and accusations to God. *How, oh my God, how can I ever come to terms with Zaeden's physical death. I miss him so much. Even having experienced the many miracles and blessings, the intense pain seems more than I can bear!*

In addition, Jim and the kids present various needs and challenges in coming to terms with our different life. I try to be strong and in tune with each of them during those ups and downs, in order to help our family through this. Some of the kids talk about Zaeden openly and happily while others walk out of the room, preferring to not talk about him at all. A couple of the kids cry freely while others are repulsed by that emotion. Turmoil results, worsened even more when Jim and I differ in opinion of how best to handle our stress-filled family life.

*Will God's peace and comfort and mercy that was gifted to our family during the desperation of the first book, ever again be present for my family?*

As the calendar moves us forward in time, the earth around us begins to change subtly and softly into the pastels of springtime. We are challenged to keep pace with the re-awakening of our surrounding landscape.

Barely six weeks after Zaeden's Celebration of Life service, I find myself kneeling with fingers in dirt, gently planting the brightly colored flowering plants into Zaeden's garden at our farm. Each of the plants has specific needs of sun or shade, spacing and height, and flowering timeframe. In this second book, I struggle along with Jim to help plant the two of us, as well as each of our kids, in a healthy family environment that nurtures our faith growth and allows each to us to bloom in our own time.

If you like this book, please go to our ministry website, www.hoflenministries.org and enter your email address so that we may contact you as soon as the second book is available. I expect publication to occur during the summer of 2012. On our website, you may also order my paintings and other books that I have published, such as "Zaeden's Rainbow" and "New Life Together".

peace,<br>lori

# Other Books Published by the Author Include...

## Zaeden's Rainbow

My two year old son, Zaeden, died in March, 2007. One of our family's favorite memories of Zaeden is his excitement in constantly pointing out colors everywhere around us.

In the biblical story of Noah and the Ark, the Rainbow is a symbol of beauty, peace, and a new beginning after Noah and his family experience a horrific flood and devastation of life as they knew it.

Our family, too, has experienced a terrible storm, but we know that Zaeden would not want us focusing on the dark walk through the Valley of the Shadow of Death.

Zaeden taught us to focus on the brilliance of life, the beautiful rainbow colors of the world around us, and sharing precious time with those we love.

## New Life Together

The life cycle story of a dragonfly nymph, who must leave his underwater friends even though he knows they are sad. They think that they will never see each other again.

After the dragonfly reaches the surface of the pond, his metamorphosis into a beautiful dragonfly allows him to swoop and soar through the air, seeing the world in a new way.

His life is not over – it is more wonderful than before. He sees his sad friends through the surface of the pond and wishes they weren't grieving for him. The dragonfly is thankful that someday they will join him and soar together in their beautiful new life together.

# About the Author

**Lori Hoflen** and husband Jim live in rural Iowa and have 11 children. They are active Christians and members of a local church.

Lori is a volunteer EMT, coaches volleyball, teaches Sunday School, and has a Master's Degree in Software Engineering. Jim is retired Air Force and works for the Department of Homeland Security.

Zaeden has a 50' x 70' fun, colorful memory garden that the family planted and lovingly cares for at the Hoflen's farm, just four miles from their house in Elk Horn, Iowa. Each of the kids has at least one area in his garden where they've placed special garden décor for Zaeden. The garden's main pathway is in the shape of a "Z", and winds through a variety of perennials and vibrant annual flowers, under shade trees and into bright sunlit areas. There are plenty of seating and relaxation areas, with whimsical wind chimes, solar lights, and bird feeders scattered throughout. Kids of all ages enjoy the water fountain and playing in the huge sandbox with toy buckets, shovels, and dump trucks.

Jim and Lori are the founders of JHL Inc., the publishing company for this book and also founders of Hoflen Ministries, a 501(c)3 non-profit organization.

**Their dream is to move their house to the farm and build a retreat center, with lodging - offering solace, comfort, and inspiration to those in need.**

# About Hoflen Ministries

www.hoflenministries.org

## What We Do
- **Speak** at support group meetings and church events
- **Publish**, both eBooks and in print
- **Gift Comfort Quilts** to those grieving a loved one's death or experiencing a challenging time
- **Provide Gardens** for meditation and retreats
- **Offer my Paintings, Sketches, and Bookmarks** for purchase to support our ministry

## How You Can Help
- Prayer
- Host and attend speaking engagements
- Donate — money, equipment, supplies

Donations are tax deductible.
Hoflen Ministries is a 501(c)3 non-profit organization.

## Who We Are
Lori Hoflen — founder, speaker and author
Jim Hoflen — technical support, administrator and publisher
Email: lori@hoflenministries.org   jim@hoflenministries.org
Mailing Address: 4314 Main Street, Elk Horn, IA 51531

www.ingramcontent.com/pod-product-compliance
Lightning Source LLC
LaVergne TN
LVHW051550070426
835507LV00021B/2507